States of Vulnerability: The Future Brain Drain of Talent to South Africa

JONATHAN CRUSH, EUGENE CAMPBELL, THUSO GREEN, SELMA NANGULAH AND HAMILTON SIMELANE

SERIES EDITOR:
PROF. JONATHAN CRUSH

SOUTHERN AFRICAN MIGRATION PROJECT
2006

Published by Idasa, 6 Spin Street, Church Square, Cape Town, 8001, and Southern African Research Centre, Queen's University, Canada.

Copyright Southern African Migration Project (SAMP) 2006
ISBN 1-920118-07-1

First published 2006
Design by Bronwen Müller
Typeset in Goudy

CONTENTS   PAGE

CHAPTER 1: VULNERABLE STATES   1

    INTRODUCTION   2

CHAPTER 2: THE POTENTIAL BRAIN DRAIN FROM BOTSWANA   8

    INTRODUCTION   9

    STUDENT PROFILE IN BOTSWANA   10

    STUDENT ATTITUDES TO EMIGRATION   11

    POLICY IMPLICATIONS   15

CHAPTER 3: THE POTENTIAL BRAIN DRAIN FROM LESOTHO   19

    INTRODUCTION   20

    STUDENT PROFILE IN LESOTHO   20

    STUDENT ATTITUDES TO EMIGRATION   22

    GOVERNMENT POLICIES   29

    CONCLUSION   29

CHAPTER 4: THE POTENTIAL BRAIN DRAIN FROM SWAZILAND   31

    INTRODUCTION   32

    STUDENT PROFILE IN SWAZILAND   32

    STUDENT ATTITUDES TO EMIGRATION   34

    GOVERNMENT POLICIES   40

CHAPTER 5: THE POTENTIAL BRAIN DRAIN FROM NAMIBIA   42

    INTRODUCTION   43

    STUDENT PROFILE IN NAMIBIA   43

    GOVERNMENT POLICIES   51

    CONCLUSION   53

ACKNOWLEDGEMENTS   54

ENDNOTES   55

MIGRATION POLICY SERIES   59

TABLES   PAGE

TABLE 1.1:   FOREIGN CITIZENS IN SOUTH AFRICA BY REGION OF ORIGIN   3

TABLE 1.2:   FOREIGN-BORN RESIDENTS OF SOUTH AFRICA, SADC COUNTRIES   4

TABLE 1.3:   LEGAL IMMIGRATION TO SOUTH AFRICA BY COUNTRY OF   4
             ORIGIN 1994-2004

TABLE 2.1:   EXPECTATIONS OF THE FUTURE IN BOTSWANA   12

TABLE 2.2:   REASONS FOR CONSIDERATION OF EMIGRATION FROM BOTSWANA   13

TABLE 2.3:   OPINIONS ABOUT LIVING CONDITIONS IN BOTSWANA AND   14
             OTHER COUNTRIES

TABLE 2.4:   COMPARISON OF BOTSWANA WITH MOST LIKELY DESTINATION   16

TABLE 2.5:   STUDENT OPINIONS ABOUT BOTSWANA GOVERNMENT POLICIES   17

TABLE 3.1:   INSTITUTIONS SURVEYED IN LESOTHO   21

TABLE 3.2:   TYPE OF SPONSORSHIP   21

TABLE 3.3:   TYPE OF SPONSORSHIP BY INSTITUTION   22

TABLE 3.4:   EXPECTATIONS OF THE FUTURE IN LESOTHO   24

TABLE 3.5:   IMPACT OF LEAVING LESOTHO ON QUALITY OF LIFE   24

TABLE 3.6:   COMPARISON OF LESOTHO AND OTHER COUNTRIES   25

TABLE 3.7:   TRAVEL EXPERIENCE OUTSIDE LESOTHO   26

TABLE 3.8:   MAJOR REASONS FOR LEAVING LESOTHO   27

TABLE 3.9:   INTENDED LENGTH OF STAY IN MLD   28

TABLE 3.10: WILLINGNESS TO CUT TIES WITH LESOTHO   29

TABLE 3.11: STUDENT OPINION ABOUT LESOTHO GOVERNMENT POLICIES   30

TABLE 3.12: STUDENT RESPONSES TO POSSIBLE RESTRICTIONS   30

TABLE 4.1:   SOURCES OF STUDENT SUPPORT   33

TABLE 4.2:   FREQUENCY OF SWAZI STUDENT TRAVEL TO SOUTH AFRICA   34

TABLE 4.3:   KNOWLEDGE OF PEOPLE WHO HAVE LEFT SWAZILAND   34

TABLE 4.4:   COMPARISON OF SWAZILAND WITH MLD   37

TABLE 4.5:   MOST IMPORTANT REASONS FOR LEAVING SWAZILAND   38

TABLE 4.6:   LIKELIHOOD OF LEAVING SWAZILAND FOR MORE THAN TWO YEARS 39

TABLE 4.7:   DESIRED LENGTH OF STAY IN MLD   40

TABLE 5.1:   TERTIARY INSTITUTIONS SAMPLED   44

TABLE 5.2:   SAMPLE BY INSTITUTION/PROGRAMME   45

TABLE 5.3:   SOURCES OF STUDENT FINANCIAL SUPPORT IN NAMIBIA   45

TABLE 5.4:   EXPECTATIONS OF THE FUTURE IN NAMIBIA   47

TABLE 5.5:   COMPARISON BETWEEN NAMIBIA AND OTHER COUNTRIES   48

TABLE 5.6:   KNOWLEDGE OF PEOPLE WHO HAVE LEFT NAMIBIA   48

TABLE 5.7:   LIKELIHOOD OF LEAVING NAMIBIA AFTER GRADUATION   49

TABLE 5.8:   COMPARISON OF NAMIBIA WITH MLD   50

TABLE 5.9:   ONGOING LINKS WITH NAMIBIA   51

TABLE 5.10: RESPONSES TO POSSIBLE RESTRICTIONS ON EMIGRATION   52

TABLE 5.11: LEVEL OF SUPPORT FOR GOVERNMENT POLICY ON EMIGRATION   52

FIGURES   PAGE

FIGURE 5.1: THE HOME LANGUAGE BREAKDOWN OF RESPONDENTS   44

EDITORIAL NOTE

This publication presents the results of SAMP's 2003 Potential Skills Base survey (PSBS) in four SADC countries. The PSBS was also implemented in South Africa and Zimbabwe. The survey results from those two countries have already appeared in the Migration Policy Series as Nos. 36 and 39. SAMP has also published an overview of the region as a whole as Migration Policy Series No. 35. SAMP wishes to thank the research teams in each of the six countries surveyed and, in particular, the managers of the studies: Eugene Campbell, Thuso Green, Hamilton Simelane, Bob Mattes, Selma Nangulah, and Dan Tevera. Wade Pendleton and Bruce Frayne played a major supporting role. Christa Schier assisted in data coordination and David Dorey and Monica Gyimah helped in the editing of this publication. Our particular thanks go to the over 10,000 students who agreed to participate in the survey and who may find it of interest to compare their views with those of other students across the SADC region.

CHAPTER 1

VULNERABLE STATES

JONATHAN CRUSH

INTRODUCTION

Skills emigration or the "brain drain" has become a major policy and research issue at the national, regional and continental level in Africa.[1] African governments emerged from colonialism with a woefully inadequate skills base. After independence, most invested heavily in skills creation, universalizing access to primary and secondary education, setting up new universities and training colleges, offering generous financial support in the form of grants and bursaries to students, and sponsoring the brightest and most promising to go overseas for advanced training. Coupled with a complementary strategy of temporary import of expatriate skills, this strategy seemed to pay off in many countries. The skills base of many countries expanded rapidly and most locally-trained citizens were absorbed into the public and private sectors.

Concerns first began to surface in the 1980s when increasing numbers of students sent overseas for further training stopped returning home and began a new life elsewhere. Then, in the 1990s, a new trend began to emerge in Southern Africa (mirroring an earlier trend in West and East Africa). Home-grown professionals began to look outside their own countries for employment. Part of this had to do with conditions at home. Certainly, economic mismanagement, political instability and civil strife made other pastures appear much greener. But externally-driven economic forces, such as Structural Adjustment Programs (SAP's), debt repayment and global trade imbalances plunged many small economies into crisis. Unemployment soared and working conditions deteriorated in country after country. The better-managed economies escaped and, as a consequence, skills tended to stay at home. On the demand side, many "developed" economies abandoned restrictionist immigration policies and actively sought out skills from other countries. In the face of falling birth rates, graying populations and (for some at least) their own brain drains, the countries of Africa presented a ripe picking field.[2]

Considerable attention is now focused on the size and impact of the African brain drain and how to develop workable retention strategies to keep skilled people at home.[3] Moral suasion appears to be having some impact through a growing number of international agreements to control recruiting and hiring of African skills. At home, governments are considering a range of options to try and persuade newly-minted skills to stay or at least stick for a while. The word from most professionals, however, is that only fundamental economic reform and a change in quality of life and economic prospects will quell the search for employment overseas.[4] To date, however, the debate has been couched very much in binary terms. The North gains and the South loses. The North poaches and the South suffers. Brain drains within the North and South receive much less attention, not because they do not exist but perhaps because the moral issues are trickier to articulate and champion.

Certain large African countries, notably South Africa and Nigeria, are suffering major losses of skilled personnel to the North.[5] They also have the potential to be major beneficiaries of an intra-continental brain drain. The temptation to recruit replacement skills from other African countries may become virtually irresistible. South Africa has resisted temptation for the best part of a decade.[6] After 1994, there were fears in many African countries that their skills base would be severely depleted by South Africa. This has not happened. According to the SA Census, the number of SADC citizens in South Africa increased by only 40,000 between 1996 and 2001.[7] The vast majority of SADC citizens in South Africa in 2001 were unskilled and semi-skilled migrants. The numbers from elsewhere in Africa only increased from 9,873 to 24,978 between 1996 and 2001, many of whom were probably refugees (Table 1.1).[8] Mozambique, Zimbabwe and Lesotho send the greatest number of migrants to South Africa, but Namibia, Swaziland and Botswana also have significant numbers of migrants in the country (Table 1.2) Table 1.3 shows that the numbers of skilled African immigrants to South Africa fell during the 1990s from most countries, and has only recently begun to increase again.

Table 1.1: Foreign Citizens in South Africa by Region of Origin		
Citizenship	1996	2001
SADC Countries	281,601	320,174
Rest of Africa	9,873	24,978
Europe	109,622	88,758
Asia	14,850	16,311
North America	5,331	5,830
Central & South America	12,902	4,761
Australia/New Zealand	2,896	2,197
Total	437,075	463,009
Source: SA Census		

The reason for the absence of a brain drain to South Africa lies primarily in that country's immigration policies post-1994. These policies were based on the assumption that immigration of any kind was a "threat" to the interests of South Africa's newly-enfranchised.[9] This argument held for the best part of the 1990s. The primary result was that the much-anticipated (and feared in source countries) flood of

Table 1.2: Foreign-Born Residents of South Africa, SADC Countries	
SADC Member State	No. Living in South Africa
Angola	11,806
Botswana	17,819
DR Congo	4,541
Lesotho	114,941
Madagascar	220
Malawi	25,090
Mauritius	3,500
Mozambique	269,669
Namibia	46,225
Swaziland	34,471
Tanzania	3,923
Zambia	23,550
Zimbabwe	131,887
Source: SA Census	

Table 1.3: Legal Immigration to South Africa by Country of Origin, 1994-2004												
SADC	1994	1995	1996	1997	1998	1999	2000	2001	2002	2003	2004	Total
Angola	2	0	7	10	9	20	0	0	0	0	0	48
Botswana	48	28	50	32	24	20	12	21	37	0	0	272
DRC	244	78	93	75	49	44	42	0	0	0	0	625
Lesotho	227	222	233	130	141	105	92	118	123	237	272	1900
Malawi	68	85	96	48	37	118	20	0	0	174	198	844
Mauritius	38	39	51	51	31	24	13	40	87	56	11	441
Mozam.	45	41	53	42	50	556	11	198	0	187	282	1465
Namibia	15	9	34	34	14	9	8	2	3	0	0	128
Swaziland	110	83	97	51	51	33	0	0	0	0	191	616
Tanzania	4	0	18	16	3	14	7	0	0	0	0	62
Zambia	75	66	69	63	72	52	38	86	101	0	140	762
Zimbabwe	556	405	394	270	300	177	88	326	464	959	1041	4980
Other Africa												
Ghana	72	0	149	151	117	74	70	0	0	248	190	1071
Kenya	38	24	47	48	81	44	34	0	0	148	149	613
Nigeria	25	45	66	77	34	40	87	198	631	1698	224	3125
Uganda	12	0	51	86	29	18	39	79	111	0	0	425

skills to South Africa did not eventuate.

Since 2000, three developments have made the prospect of a brain drain to South Africa far more likely. First, the ANC government has become convinced that the country is unable to contain its own skills brain drain and is in the midst of a "skills crisis." A more open immigration policy is therefore needed. Although it is an extremely cumbersome piece of legislation, the 2002 Immigration Act (as amended in 2004) has, as an avowed outcome, easing the import of skills from outside the country.[10] Second, a SADC Draft Protocol on the Facilitation of Movement of Persons has recently been ratified by six countries, including South Africa.[11] The Protocol was first mooted as long ago as 1995 and has remained on the drawing board for a decade, largely because of South African opposition.[12] South Africa's change of position is consistent with the new openness towards immigration. The Protocol, when in force, should make it easier for skilled people from the rest of SADC to work in South Africa (and vice-versa). Third, political and economic conditions in a number of neighbouring states (notably Zimbabwe) continue to deteriorate. The number of skilled Zimbabweans (and other SADC citizens) moving to South Africa has recently begun to escalate.[13]

Just because South Africa opens its doors, it does not automatically follow that everyone will automatically go through them. In the late 1990s, SAMP undertook surveys of working professionals in a number of SADC states and found that there was a high, though country-specific, level of interest in relocating.[14] The SAMP Potential Skills Base Survey (PSBS), implemented in 2003, attempted to project this scenario into the future. What are today's students thinking about their future? Is emigration a part of their plans? Are they satisfied with things at home or are they likely to leave at the first available opportunity? And, if they do leave, will they return and/or retain strong links while they are gone?

The PSBS was conducted in six SADC countries (Botswana, Lesotho, Namibia, South Africa, Swaziland and Zimbabwe). Over 10,000 final year students in universities, technical colleges and other higher education institutions across the region were interviewed. The regional picture that emerged showed considerable variation from country to country in the emigration potential of SADC students. As the summary report, *Degrees of Uncertainty*, concluded:

> The emigration potential of SADC students on graduation
> is high and economic factors are paramount when students
> consider what to do in the future. The primary losers from
> the brain drain of new skills are likely to be Zimbabwe,
> Swaziland and Lesotho. The primary beneficiaries are likely

> to be North America and Europe and, within the region,
> South Africa and Botswana. South Africa, at the same
> time, is likely to be both a victim and a beneficiary of the
> brain drain.[15]

This rather sobering conclusion draws attention to the fundamental contradiction that lies at the heart of policy responses to the brain drain. The fact is that SADC is a regional grouping of states of which one, South Africa, is by far the most powerful economically and offers better wages and working conditions to skilled people than anywhere else. If the policy and legislative gates that made it difficult to legally emigrate to South Africa during the 1990s now swing open, the rush from poorer neighbouring countries could become overwhelming. The impact on the public service and private sector in South Africa's neighbours could be catastrophic.

Against this backdrop, SAMP's PSBS findings in these states become of considerable interest. How do tomorrow's skilled professionals in small countries such as Botswana, Lesotho, Namibia and Swaziland view life in their own country? How satisfied are they with conditions and prospects at home? What comparisons do they make between life at home and a prospective new life across the border in South Africa? How strongly does South Africa feature in their emigration plans? What measures could their home governments take to encourage them to stay? Those are the obvious questions raised by the PSBS and addressed in this policy paper.

The other set of concerns is prompted by the decision to publish four case studies in a single volume. Not only does this provide important opportunities for comparison between four vulnerable states, but it also allows policy makers in each state to take stock of the particular situation and case-specific challenges that they face. The four countries chosen are all small (in terms of population size) and highly vulnerable to "poaching" and skills loss to South Africa. Historically, they are all heavily integrated into the South African economy and labour market (for example, there were no border controls between BLS and South Africa before 1963). Citizens of the BLS states also share many cultural similarities and family ties with Tswana, Sesotho and SiSwati-speaking South Africans.

Botswana has much the strongest economy of the four and hitherto has probably offered better employment prospects to its new graduates.[16] Lesotho has a long tradition of migration to South Africa and much poorer, though fluctuating, employment prospects for new graduates.[17] Swaziland's economy is in serious trouble and the prospects for new graduates are probably dimmer than at any time since Independence.[18] Namibia has virtually no history of skilled, black, migration to South

Africa. That may be about to change as more and more Namibian students take up places at South African universities and the friction of distance between the two countries is reduced through air travel.[19]

This publication demonstrates that despite many differences, new graduates in all four countries will emerge with degrees and certificates that they also see as passports to better jobs and standards of living in South Africa (and abroad). Nearby South Africa is still the destination of choice for newly-minted graduates in these countries. Given the changing attitudes in South Africa towards immigration and the imminent lowering of the obstacles to skilled migrants, the governments of these four countries face a potentially critical situation. The HIV/AIDS epidemic is already eating away at their professional classes. An intraregional brain drain will only exacerbate the crisis. True, many emigrants will retain strong links with home but this needs to be encouraged not assumed. But fundamentally, only economic reform and growth is going to keep people at home. This publication is designed to sound the alarm rather than provide solutions.

Governments face an uphill struggle if they are going to keep students at home, capitalize on their desire to serve, and recoup their investment in skills development. Failing that, governments should be letting down their own drawbridges, taking advantage of the new global mobility of skilled professionals and importing skills trained elsewhere. They truly ought to be considering that already. If nothing else, the findings in this publication should prompt serious reflection on the viability of continuing with the nationalistic, restrictive immigration and migration policies that have characterized Southern Africa since the 1960s.

Chapter 2

The Potential Brain Drain from Botswana

Eugene K. Campbell

INTRODUCTION

Since the 1970s, the Botswana government has invested heavily in human resource development.[20] The highest proportion of recurrent expenditure in the national budget is in the educational sector (30% in 2003-4, compared with only 7% on health). Post-independence educational investment led to the rapid expansion of primary and secondary education. Between 1985 and 1991, for example, secondary school enrolment increased from 38% to 65% of eligible children. Admission to degree programmes at the University of Botswana increased by almost 150% over the same period. Students studying subjects not offered at the University of Botswana were sponsored by the government to study in Europe and the USA. With very few exceptions, Batswana who studied outside the country were happy to return home and contribute to the country's healthy economy.

Government is more involved in funding tertiary education than in any other SADC state. Eighty eight percent of students are on government bursaries (with only 14% not involving some form of payback). Conversely, Batswana students have one of the lowest levels of family and individual financial support. Botswana also demands more payback in terms of public service than the government of any other country (53% of bursaries compared to a regional average of only 31%).

Unlike other countries in Southern Africa, Botswana does not have a history of skilled emigration.[21] However, for the first time there are signals of an imminent brain drain from the country. In 2002, the Botswana Minister of Health declared the situation an emergency, and appealed to health professionals to be patriotic and stay to help improve the health status of the population at home. Ironically, a few months later, the Minister himself resigned and left for Europe to work with the United Nations.

Botswana frequently receives international commendation for its economic policies and rapid growth in the 1980s and 1990s. Botswana is among only a handful of countries in sub-Saharan Africa with vibrant economies.[22] Before the 1990s, university students were practically guaranteed jobs on graduation. By the mid-1990s, it was increasingly obvious that government was unable to implement a policy of full employment for university graduates. Inevitably, government's policy of recruiting experienced skilled migrants from outside the country was resented as a major source of graduate unemployment.[23] The prospect and experience of unemployment, plus the increasingly ostentatious display of wealth by the employed, have served to inflate aspirations, expectations and tastes.

Botswana has always recognized the importance of importing skills (brain gain) and training (brain train) in a way that makes it unique in the region. However, if jobs for all Batswana cannot be guaranteed, it is inevitable that resentment against foreigners will increase. Indeed, the evidence suggests that the tide has already turned and skilled non-nationals are feeling increasingly unwelcome.[24] The other consequence of the absence of guaranteed employment is that Batswana are going to become more interested in leaving the country and use their locally-acquired skills to market themselves internationally. A decade ago, a study of this nature would probably have revealed little interest amongst students in leaving the country. This chapter sets out to discover if this situation has changed, and if so, to suggest reasons why this might be.

STUDENT PROFILE IN BOTSWANA

The PSBS study in Botswana surveyed a representative sample of final year students in tertiary training institutions. The survey was conducted between October 2002 and January 2003. With the exception of a few non-accredited health institutions, the University of Botswana and all health and teacher training institutes were included in the survey. The institutions surveyed included the University of Botswana (UB) and Botswana College of Education (BCA), Botswana Institute of Accounting and Commerce (BIAC), Institutes of Health Sciences in Gaborone, Lobatse, Serowe and Francistown, and Colleges of Education in Tlokweng, Lobatse, Serowe, Tonota and Francistown. Initially, the health and teacher training institutes in Molepolole were included but, due to difficulties in reaching students, they were eventually excluded from the study.

The sample was drawn from the cluster of final year students and the proportion (25% of the total) is reasonably large. Out of 1,201 students interviewed, 63% (756) were female and 37% (445) male. Forty-three percent were less than 24 years of age. About 78% spoke mostly Setswana at home, and the rest Kalanga. The majority were studying in Certificate or Diploma programmes (45%) or in Bachelors degree programmes (41%). Less than 10% were studying for Master's degrees. Some 62% of students were either in teacher training colleges or in Faculties of Social Sciences and Humanities at the University of Botswana.

Females dominated the liberal arts and political and administration areas, while males dominated the sciences. Nearly all (95%) were full-time students. Over three quarters were sponsored by the national government, with greater levels of sponsorship given to younger female students. The conditions of government sponsorship require them to work for the government for at least a short time after graduating. About one-third of the sponsorships had no condition attached.

Botswana has invested heavily in female education in the last two decades and the sample derived for this study was therefore female-dominated. An important issue raised by this finding is whether there is any gender difference in proclivity to stay or emigrate. The question is whether males and females are acquiring internationally marketable skills equally. Nursing, for example, is a heavily female-dominated profession in Botswana and African nurses are certainly in demand in Europe. On the other hand, are females accessing "professional" and science-based degrees in the same proportions as men or are they still "ghettoized" in the social sciences and humanities? These are important questions because all forms of higher education do not make students equally mobile.

STUDENT ATTITUDES TO EMIGRATION

Batswana students identify very strongly with their country. The vast majority (93%) were proud to be citizens and almost 90% said they would want their children to consider themselves Batswana. Virtually all (95%) expressed a strong desire to assist with economic and social development in the country. Around three quarters (77%) believe that they have a very important role to play in the future development of Botswana. This is education-specific, with the degree of enthusiasm falling as the educational level increases.

Despite the general health of the Botswana economy, however, only 17% of the students are satisfied or very satisfied with their current economic circumstances. There is no significant difference between males and females. However, nearly 70% anticipate that their personal economic circumstances will be better or much better five years hence. This expression of hope is significantly influenced by expected level of educational achievement on completion of their studies. Males are certainly more optimistic about their economic future than females.

The anticipation of a brighter personal future is positively correlated with perceptions of the current and future well-being of the national economy. Nevertheless, the students are not as optimistic about the future of the national economy. Just 38% are satisfied or very satisfied with the current state of the economy and only 42% feel things will be better or much better in five years' time. These attitudes are partly explained by a loss of confidence in the ability of the government to provide an environment of full employment for graduates. Over 80% think that the government has not done enough to ease graduate unemployment. Only 14% anticipate an improvement in the prospect of finding a desirable job after graduating and just 21% anticipate improvement in the conditions for personal advancement.

The majority of students are not particularly positive about future socio-economic conditions in the country (Table 2.1). Over 60% expect that the cost of living, job availability, taxation, housing availability and the HIV/AIDS epidemic will get worse. On no single social or economic indicator do a majority of students feel that the situation will improve (although a significant minority are confident of improvements in income, the quality of public services and the availability of quality affordable products). Less than 40% are optimistic about future prospects of finding good schools in Botswana for children or good medical services for the family.

Table 2.1: Expectations of the Future in Botswana.			
Expectation of the Future (%)			
Socio-Economic Condition in 5 years	Better	Same	Worse
Cost of living	20.4	12.7	66.9
Ability to find job I want	13.6	12.9	73.4
Prospect for professional advancement	27.9	22.5	49.6
HIV/AIDS situation	21.3	9.5	69.1
Job security	27.1	35.7	37.2
Income level	47.3	24.8	27.9
Ability of find desirable house	22.8	14.6	62.6
Ability to find good school for children	37.5	23.8	38.7
Ability to find medical services for family	38.7	25.5	35.8
Fair taxation	11.8	29.3	59.0
Personal Safety	23.9	28.4	47.7
Family's safety	24.1	29.8	46.1
Future of children	38.9	21.3	39.8
Quality upkeep of public amenities	40.2	26.5	33.3
Availability of affordable quality products	40.6	25.8	33.6
Customer Service	40.1	28.7	31.2
N=1,201			

Due to a recent increase in crime (including physical and sexual assault, house breaking and robbery), perceptions of personal safety have declined considerably since the late 1990s. Almost 50% of students expect personal security to get worse in the future; only 29% of working professionals felt the same when this question was asked in 1998.[25]

Does the level of student dissatisfaction translate into an interest in or desire to leave the country? Almost a quarter (22%) say they intend to leave Botswana within six months of graduation. There is no significant difference between males and females. Nor are intentions influenced by level of educational attainment or type of programme. The proportion of potential emigrants increases to 40% within two years, and 51% within five. More than half of all students say they are likely to live and work outside Botswana for a short period of time. Around half (49%) believe that they could easily find employment in their most likely destination (MLD). Males are more certain than females about this. About 46% of students say they cannot afford the cost of emigrating to their MLD.

Table 2.2 shows the proportion of students who have considered emigration who give a particular reason for wanting to emigrate (including the primary reasons and the average of the primary, secondary and tertiary (PST) reasons). Again, there is no significant difference between male and female answers. Income levels are cited most often (38% as the primary reason and 23% on average). Job availability is next, followed by prospects for professional advancement. On average, professional advancement is marginally more important than job availability. Housing, consumer service, quality of public amenities and

Table 2.2: Reasons for Consideration of Emigration from Botswana		
Reason	Primary Reason (%)	Average of PST Reasons (%)
Cost of living	16.7	11.9
Ability to find job	13.6	9.9
Prospect for professional advancement	13.4	14.0
HIV/AIDS situation	3.7	3.9
Job security	2.4	3.7
Income level	37.9	22.9
Ability to find house	0.3	1.9
Good school for children	2.9	7.5
Medical service for family	1.4	5.4
Fair taxation level	1.7	2.3
Personal safety	1.6	2.9
Family's safety	0.9	1.6
Future of children in Botswana	1.3	3.8
Quality of public amenities	0.7	1.9
Affordable quality product	1.1	4.4
Customer service	0.3	2.0
Total	100.0	100.0
Note: PST = primary, secondary and tertiary.		
N=699		

family safety have very little influence. Very few cite the HIV/AIDS epidemic in the country as a reason for leaving despite the likely economic impact of the disease. The rate of increase in gross domestic product (GDP) is projected to halve by 2010 (falling from 4.3% to 2.4%), poverty to increase by up to 6%, and household per capita income to fall by up to 10%.[26]

About 80% of the students feel they would be better off living in Europe, North America or Australia/New Zealand than in Botswana (see Table 2.3). South Africa was a distant second, with almost half (49%) thinking it would be better to live there than in Botswana. Students in Botswana have a low opinion of the quality of life within other countries in the SADC. Male students are generally more positive than female students about conditions in South Africa.

Table 2.3: Opinions about Living Conditions in Botswana and Other Countries.						
Other country compared to Botswana	Anticipated Living Condition					
	Better		Same		Worse	
	Male	Female	Male	Female	Male	Female
Lesotho	24.9	26.5	34.4	37.7	40.7	35.8
Mozambique	11.8	10.9	17.5	23.2	70.7	65.8
Namibia	21.3	21.5	47.9	47.7	30.8	30.8
Swaziland	18.8	18.4	37.4	42.2	43.8	39.5
Zimbabwe	7.1	6.6	5.4	5.6	87.5	87.9
South Africa	53.5	46.3	31.2	27.5	15.3	26.1
Angola	14.4	10.3	17.7	26.4	67.9	63.3
Malawi	10.7	9.5	29.7	27.5	59.6	63.0
Zambia	9.5	8.7	15.1	21.3	75.4	70.0
East Africa	13.4	15.5	24.5	20.3	62.1	64.2
West Africa	14.8	16.9	19.6	19.4	65.6	63.7
Central Africa	11.2	14.7	25.7	25.3	63.1	60.0
North Africa	27.7	20.4	30.4	25.4	41.9	54.0
Europe	82.0	79.9	11.2	10.2	6.8	9.9
North America	79.6	80.3	11.3	10.1	9.7	9.6
Australia / New Zealand	79.1	77.8	12.4	13.0	8.5	9.2
Asia / China	54.2	45.2	21.8	23.1	24.0	31.7

Among those who are considering leaving, North America is the MLD (33%). Europe is a close second (31%), while South Africa is the third choice. The least preferred destinations are elsewhere in Africa and Asia.

Overwhelmingly, students of both sexes believe that income levels are better in their MLD than in Botswana (Table 2.4). More males than females anticipate a better cost of living in the MLD. Both believe that prospects for professional advancement are much better in the MLD. The MLD predictably features better on just about every economic measure. Botswana only features significantly better in the area of personal and family safety.

Would Botswana's new graduates leave temporarily or permanently? Only 11% say they would want to be away for less than one year. The peak preferred duration of stay in the MLD (42%) is two to five years. However, nearly a third (29%) say they would opt for a more permanent departure (greater than five years). Males are significantly more interested in long duration emigration than females. Over a third say they would want to become permanent residents of their MLD; a stronger sentiment among males than females. Over a quarter want citizenship in the MLD (again, more males than females). The same proportion of students say they would prefer to retire in the MLD. These findings certainly indicate significant interest among a minority of students in leaving Botswana for good.

POLICY IMPLICATIONS

The government of Botswana has a potentially significant problem on its hands. Despite high levels of commitment to the country and an expectation of a reasonably bright personal and general economic future, there is significant interest in leaving the country. Europe and North America are the preferred destinations but South Africa also emerges as a potentially significant destination for the newly-skilled.

What options are available to government to retain new graduates? Students themselves have strong opinions about what would and would not work. Over half (59%) would find it justified if the government of Botswana required citizens to complete some form of non-military national service before enrolling in a tertiary educational institution (Table 2.5). Significantly more males than females shared this view. Just under half (47%) think it would be justified if they were required to work in the country after completing their studies. Given the high-level of tied sponsorship in Botswana, this suggests a certain amount of disgruntlement with having to "pay back" in the form of public service.

The survey showed that even if the government were to implement a policy that made it difficult to emigrate, 28% of students would still proceed to live and work outside Botswana. A requirement of one year of national service would actually encourage a third of students to

Table 2.4: Comparison of Botswana with Most Likely Destination		Opinion		
		Better in Botswana	Same	Better in MLD
Cost of living	Male	37.4	13.2	49.4
	Female	46.7	12.0	41.3
Ability to find a job	Male	32.0	19.2	48.8
	Female	40.9	21.3	37.8
Prospect for professional advancement	Male	20.5	13.8	65.7
	Female	23.1	19.2	57.7
HIV / AIDS situation	Male	6.8	24.2	69.0
	Female	13.3	30.9	55.8
Job security	Male	37.0	22.4	40.6
	Female	40.2	23.5	36.3
Income level	Male	13.2	10.4	76.4
	Female	14.6	12.4	73.0
Ability to find house	Male	24.6	17.7	57.7
	Female	28.6	20.6	50.8
Good school for children	Male	18.8	12.9	68.3
	Female	23.6	16.1	60.3
Medial service for family	Male	20.4	16.3	63.3
	Female	26.9	16.4	56.7
Fair taxation level	Male	34.7	27.5	37.8
	Female	34.7	31.7	33.6
Personal safety	Male	53.5	17.2	29.3
	Female	48.3	22.8	28.9
Family's safety	Male	55.5	17.9	26.6
	Female	52.7	21.2	26.1
Future of children in Botswana	Male	36.1	17.5	46.4
	Female	39.7	19.5	40.8
Quality of public amenities	Male	15.1	12.9	72.0
	Female	16.6	17.4	66.0
Affordable quality product	Male	11.5	11.3	77.2
	Female	16.0	14.7	69.3
Customer service	Male	11.1	17.4	71.5
	Female	16.6	24.0	59.4
N = 1,201				

Table 2.5: Student Opinions about Botswana Government Policies						
	Justified (%)		Neither (%)		Unjustified (%)	
	Male	Female	Male	Female	Male	Female
Require citizens to complete some form of national/public service before enrolling at institutions of higher learning	59.9	57.5	10.4	8.2	29.7	34.3
Require citizens who have received government bursaries for education to complete some form of national service	57.7	57.9	9.3	9.3	33.0	32.8
Require citizens to work in Lesotho for several years after completion of their education	52.1	43.9	10.1	11.1	37.8	45.0
N = 1,201						

emigrate. Generally, policies designed to restrict emigration are therefore likely to defer but not stop the implementation of emigration intentions. If the government were to implement measures to encourage the return of qualified professionals from abroad, 70% of students would be in favour. The general opinion (78%) is that emigration will not abate if the government does nothing to encourage highly skilled professionals to stay.

A solution to the threatened brain drain in Botswana does not lie in policies to try and directly dissuade new graduates from leaving. Rather it lies in government's ability to demonstrate that it is actively working towards implementing a massive economic development policy. About 88% of students feel that a vigorous economic drive by the government would encourage Batswana professionals to stay and work in the country. Presently, the national economy does not have the capacity to absorb all graduates. The new thinking among educated youths is that the only other viable options are self-employment and international employment. The educated population in Botswana is becoming increasingly aware of its need to maximize its international marketability. The emigration option, consequently, has become increasingly popular in student discourse and thinking.

The government could institute a programme to encourage professionals now working in developed countries to return home. It could also revert to the impractical pre-1990 policy of assuring full employment for citizen graduates. The question is: would the cost of this outweigh the socioeconomic benefits of skill retention? The answer must be negative. Botswana's economic survival rests heavily on the dictates of the global economy within which reliance on diamonds and beef exports has fostered international trade links. The benefits of globalization necessitate considerable compromise on migration. Even if immigration of non-citizens was actually a significant factor in unemployment and lowered incomes among skilled citizens, it should be recognized as a small price to pay for sustained national economic prosperity.

There is an inherent problem with the rate of professional progression in Botswana, stemming from a conflict between exaggerated aspirations and reality. There is a widespread belief in the existence of unlimited job opportunities at senior professional levels for skilled citizens who can easily displace expatriates. However, most expatriates are highly experienced and government does not intend to, and nor should it, localize positions at the expense of production efficiency simply to appease the growing anti-foreign sentiment in the country. At the same time, these sentiments should not remain unchecked. If the government wishes to retain its emphasis on importing needed skills, it needs to explain to citizens why this continues to be necessary.[27]

Chapter 3

The Potential Brain Drain from Lesotho

Thuso Green

INTRODUCTION

Lesotho has a long history of supplying unskilled and semi-skilled migrants to South African mines, towns and farms.[28] With the end of apartheid, new job opportunities have opened up in South Africa for skilled Basotho. Entry to South Africa is easy and many are able, though strong family and other connections, to obtain the necessary employment and residence documentation.[29] South Africa itself takes a relatively relaxed attitude to Basotho working in the country. Despite more general reluctance to hire skilled foreigners, it has allowed employers to hire people from Lesotho with the requisite skills. The 2001 Census showed that there were 114,941 Lesotho-born people in South Africa.[30] Amongst them are growing numbers of skilled people including teachers, nurses and public servants. Many Basotho also occupy prominent positions in the South African private and public sectors.

Further study is needed of the scope and impact of the brain drain from Lesotho.[31] One of the key questions is whether the new skilled migrants are reproducing the migrant behaviour of their unskilled counterparts, using Lesotho as a base for temporary forays into the South African labour market. Another is what kinds of links skilled professionals retain with home. Are they significant remitters and investors in their home country or are they in the process of cutting economic ties? A related question is whether Basotho still see South Africa as their most likely destination or are they, like professionals in other SADC countries, now looking further afield, to Europe and North America. Then there is the critical policy question of whether the Lesotho government is investing in skills development for the benefit of South Africa. Like every other country faced with temporary or permanent emigration of its citizens, Lesotho needs to develop retention and return strategies. Finally, there is the related issue of future trends and developments. What form will the brain drain take in the future? What kinds of links will migrants retain with home? Should the government be encouraging more immigration to meet skills shortfalls caused by out-migration?

STUDENT PROFILE IN LESOTHO

The Lesotho survey was carried out at eight institutions in all (Table 3.1). Forty three percent of those interviewed were doing undergraduate degrees at the National University of Lesotho. Most of the remainder were undertaking certificate or diploma studies in various sectors include industry, education, health and agriculture. The majority (92%) were full time students. Nearly two-thirds (64%) of those interviewed were female, confirming that females in Lesotho are generally more likely to progress to tertiary education than males. The age range varied from 18 to 52 years, with an average age of 25. The majority (69%) were still single while about a quarter (25%) were married. The rest were separated (1%), divorced (0.9%), abandoned (2%), widowed (2%) or cohabiting (2%). The mean number of dependents was 3.7, with females having more dependents than males.

Table 3.1: Institutions Surveyed in Lesotho		
Institution	District	No.
National University of Lesotho (NUL)	Maseru	446
Lesotho College of Education (LCE)	Maseru	266
Lerotholi Technical Institute (LTI)	Maseru	119
Centre of Accounting Studies (CAS)	Maseru	60
National Health Training Centre (NHTC)	Maseru	43
Catholic Technical School of Leribe (CTS)	Leribe	41
Agricultural College (Leribe campus) (AC)	Leribe	32
Institute of Extra Mural Studies (IEMS)	Maseru	29
Total		1,129

The vast majority of students self-identified as members of poorer economic strata (66% "lower class" and working class). About a quarter say they are "middle-class." Higher education is therefore still a potential route out of poverty for many families. Almost half come from a rural communal area. Only 12% come from Maseru and the remainder are from other large or small towns.

Table 3.2: Type of sponsorship		
Type of sponsorship	No.	%
Government bursary (some payment required)	902	79.9
Private/family funds	96	8.5
Government scholarship	71	6.3
University bursary (some payment required)	18	1.6
Technicon bursary (some payment required)	11	1
Private scholarship	9	0.8
University scholarship (no payment pay back required)	8	0.7
Technicon scholarship (no payment pay back required)	7	0.6
Bank/study loan	6	0.5
Tuition waver as member on NUL staff	1	0.1
Total	1,129	100

Given the general poverty of the population and poor socio-economic background of many students, it is unsurprising that government is heavily involved in sponsorship of tertiary education (Table 3.3). As many as 900 students (79.9%) have government bursaries with conditions attached. Fewer than 100 draw on personal or family funds and even fewer have bank loans.

Table 3.3: Type of sponsorship by institution								
Type of sponsorship	Name of institution							
	CAS	NHTC	NUL	LCE	AC	CTS	LTI	IEMS
Government scholarship (no payback required)	4	1	36	17	2	6	3	2
Government bursary (some payback required)	56	43	396	237	30	4	113	23
University scholarship (no payback required)	0	0	3	2	0	0	0	3
University bursary (some payback required)	0	1	6	8	0	0	3	0
Technicon scholarship (no payback required)	0	0	2	1	0	4	0	0
Technicon bursary (some payback required)	1	1	0	6	0	1	2	0
Personal/family funds	8	4	32	19	1	25	9	0
Private scholarship	2	0	3	1	0	2	1	0
Bank/study loan	0	0	1	1	0	0	3	1
Tuition waiver NUL staff	0	0	1	0	0	0	0	0

Student Attitudes to Emigration

Students in Lesotho do not make decisions about whether to stay or leave in a vacuum. While the precise numbers of skilled people who have already left Lesotho are unknown, today's students are certainly very aware, from personal experience, that many have gone before them. Just over 40% have immediate family members who have left Lesotho permanently. The figure for those who have extended family members and friends who have left is as high as 63%. When it comes to colleagues or co-workers, the findings are equally dramatic. Sixty seven percent of students at university and 64% in certificate or diploma training courses know colleagues or co-workers who have left the country. Around a third of all students say that "most" or "almost all" have left the country.

As in many other countries of the region, there is a basic tension between identity and material reality. Like students elsewhere, Basotho are fiercely nationalistic.[32] Over 90% are proud to be called Basotho and would want their children to feel the same way. But is living in Lesotho a natural corollary? The majority of students (80%) feel that they have an important role to play in the future of Lesotho. And over 90% express a desire to help build Lesotho and feel it their "duty" to contribute their skills and talents to the country. However, as many as 59% also feel that citizenship does not matter as long as one has a good quality of life. In other words, loyalty to the idea of being Basotho may be conditional. How deep does loyalty run? Under what circumstances would material reality trump idealism and patriotism? What might induce students to look for a better quality of life elsewhere?

Since economic circumstances play a major role in the migration decisions of skilled people, perceptions of personal and national economic health are a good starting point. However, nearly three-quarters of the student body are either strongly dissatisfied or dissatisfied with their current economic status. Most have a positive outlook on the future with 68% feeling that in five years their personal economic status will have improved. The question that is uppermost in their minds is whether they can realize these dreams within Lesotho or whether leaving the country is a necessary part of improving their circumstances.

How optimistic are students about the general economic future of Lesotho? Over 90% are dissatisfied with current economic conditions in the country. Regarding the future, there is an equal split between those who think that national economic performance will improve and those who think that it will deteriorate over the next five years. On more specific measures there tends to be a 2:1 split: future cost of living (45% worse v 23% better), income levels (44% worse v 27% better), taxation levels (48% worse v 19% better) and ability to find a desirable job (50% worse v 28% better) (Table 3.4). Students are a little more optimistic about their prospects for professional advancement (27% v 36%) and job security (29% v 39%). They are fairly equally divided on the prospects for "social" and "safety" issues such as finding a desirable house, good schools, medical services and family security. However, on most critical economic measures almost half of Basotho students clearly believe that conditions will deteriorate in the future. This is a very large pool of negative sentiment that could potentially also believe that it is only by leaving the country that a desirable level of employment and income can be achieved.

The majority of students (75%) think that those who have left Lesotho permanently are better off than when they were in Lesotho (Table 3.5). In other words, students do tend to see leaving as a

Table 3.4: Expectations of the Future in Lesotho (%)			
	Expectation of the Future (%)		
Socio-Economic Condition in 5 Years	Better	Same	Worse
Cost of living	23.3	25.4	45.7
Ability to find the right job	27.7	15.3	50.2
Prospects for professional advancement	33.7	26.5	27.1
Job Security	39	20.3	28.8
Level of income	27.2	20.5	43.8
Ability to find the right house	29	21.1	39.5
Ability to find a good school for children	44.3	22.8	27.3
Ability to find medical services for family/children	37.8	23.3	34
A level of fair taxation	18.8	20.7	48.5
Personal safety	32.7	19.8	37.8
Family's safety	33.8	20.1	35
Future of children in Lesotho	36.3	18.9	35.2
Quality upkeep of public amenities	23.2	18.9	47.4
Availability of affordable quality products	27.7	21.3	42
Customer service	29.7	22.4	40.8
N = 1,129			

potential way to improve their own quality of life, particularly in light of the widespread belief that economic conditions in Lesotho itself are not going to improve. The question is whether the simple act of relocating will impact positively on quality of life or whether they think this depends on where they go.

Table 3.5: Impact of Leaving Lesotho on Quality of Life		
Quality of life of those who have left Lesotho	No.	%
Much better	526	50.8
Better	246	23.7
About the same	109	10.5
Worse	35	3.4
Much Worse	22	2.1
Don't Know	98	9.5
Total	1036	100.0

Asked to compare the situation in Lesotho with neighbouring SADC countries and other parts of the world, almost a third say they have no knowledge of other parts of Africa and some SADC countries such as Angola and Malawi. Fifteen to twenty percent would not venture an opinion on North America and Europe. Less than five percent, however, are unfamiliar with South Africa and Botswana (Table 3.6). Both of these countries are seen as places that do much better than Lesotho. Nearly 80% say that Botswana and South Africa are better or much better than Lesotho. The figures for other countries in SADC are much lower: for example, Mozambique (15%), Malawi (16%), Zambia (19%), Zimbabwe (19%), Namibia (25%), and Swaziland (32%). While Lesotho does not compare favourably with either Europe or North America in the minds of students, South Africa and Botswana are definitely also seen as best off in comparison with home.

Table 3.6: Comparison of Lesotho and Other Countries						
Better or Worse than Lesotho (%)	Much Better	Better	About the same	Worse	Much Worse	Don't know
Botswana	42.6	36.2	13.8	2.6	1.1	3.8
Mozambique	4.0	11.4	27.3	24.6	14.4	18.3
Namibia	5.4	19.3	33.3	14.1	5.1	22.7
Swaziland	8.2	23.4	40.5	11.8	4.7	11.3
Zimbabwe	6.6	12.0	17.6	22.5	26.3	15
South Africa	43.1	33.9	12.3	3.5	2.7	4.6
Angola	5.0	16.0	27.9	13.7	8.8	28.6
Malawi	3.9	11.8	27.9	17.0	9.7	29.8
Zambia	3.8	15.0	29.1	13.5	8.2	30.4
East Africa	5.2	15.9	23.0	14.4	8.0	33.5
West Africa	4.3	18.0	23.8	12.9	7.0	33.7
Central Africa	6.4	17.3	21.7	13.1	9.0	32.3
North Africa	9.2	21.5	20.8	10.2	5.8	32.1
Europe	53.7	15.8	8.7	3.9	3.5	14.4
North America	51.5	18.7	7.5	4.7	4.0	13.5
Australia/ New Zealand	43.7	22.2	10.0	4.2	3.1	16.8
Asia/China	29.6	22.7	11.1	8.7	10.2	17.6
N = 1,129						

More than half of the students (57%) say that if they were to leave Lesotho, they would prefer to live in South Africa. Nearly a third (31%) believe that they will end up in South Africa. This is followed by those who say they will most likely go to Botswana (25%), the United Kingdom (10%), Europe (9%) and the United State of America (7%). While the emigration horizons of Basotho students seem to be lifting, the majority are still not looking beyond a future in South Africa.

Opinions about countries such as South Africa are based primarily on personal experience. Over 80% of students travel to another country in Southern Africa at least once or twice a year (35% more than once a month) (Table 3.7). Travel experience of other parts of Africa and elsewhere is extremely limited. Data from other SAMP studies suggests that a large majority of people from Lesotho travel to South Africa for a variety of reasons but mainly for shopping, school and medical services.[33] Visits to other parts of the world are very limited for all but a few respondents.

Table 3.7: Travel Experience Outside Lesotho						
Frequency	Southern Africa (%)	Elsewhere in Africa (%)	Europe (%)	North America (%)	Australia/ New Zealand (%)	Asia (%)
More than once a month	34.7	2.4	0.3	0.2	0.1	0.7
Once a month	14.6	3.3	0.3	0.2	0.2	0.1
Once every few months	22.0	4.6	0.6	0.4	0.6	0.5
Once or twice a year	10.1	8.3	0.9	0.2	0.4	0.6
Once every few years	6.7	10.7	1.1	0.8	0.4	0.5
Just once or twice	5.6	11.7	1.7	1.0	0.6	0.4
Never	6.3	59.0	95.2	97.3	97.8	97.3
Total	100	100	100	100	100	100
N = 1,129						

How likely are today's Basotho students to follow their unskilled counterparts out of the country? The survey found that 43% of respondents have given moving to another country a great deal of consideration while another (34%) have given it some consideration. Only 18% have not considered it at all. Given that there is an acute shortage of nurses in Lesotho, it is a great concern that 76% of final-year students at the National Health Training Centre are considering leaving. While consideration of leaving is an important first-step, likelihood of doing so is a more accurate measure of intentions. Over a third (35%) of the students said it was likely or very likely they would leave within six months of graduation (rising to 56% within two years of graduation).

Students were asked for the three most important reasons why they might actually leave. The most popular reasons were job security (mentioned by 23%), finding a suitable job (21%), cost of living (21%) and prospects for professional advancement (8%). Interestingly, only 2% mentioned income and 2% taxation levels as a reason to leave. These two factors were only marginally more important as second and third choice reasons for leaving. Job security and finding the right job were the most important reasons overall (Table 3.8) with income even rating below ability to find the right house, children's schooling, family safety and the HIV/AIDS situation. In sum, Basotho students seem more concerned about secure employment than levels of income per se. Given the volatile nature of the Lesotho labour market, this is perhaps not all that surprising.

Table 3.8: Major Reason for Leaving Lesotho	
Reasons	% of responses
Job security	17.4
Ability to find the right job	12.5
Cost of living	9.9
Prospects for professional advancement	8.9
Ability to find the right house	8.8
Family safety	5.7
Ability to find a good school for children	5.3
HIV/AIDS situation	4.8
Personal safety	4.6
Level of income	4.4
Quality upkeep of public amenities	3.9
Your fair level of taxation	3.1
Ability to find medical services for children	2.7
Availability of affordable quality production	2.7
The future of children in Lesotho	2.5
Customer service	0.1

More than half the students (56%) think the cost of living is much better or better in their Most Likely Destination (MLD) than in Lesotho. When it comes to finding the right job, 56% say that they have a much better or better chance in the MLD than in Lesotho. Prospects for job advancement are also said to be much better than in Lesotho by 62% of students. Similarly, job security is thought to be much better in the MLD than in Lesotho. A large proportion (61%) feel that the level of income in the MLD is better than in Lesotho. A very small proportion (16%) think that the chance to get a good school for children is better in Lesotho than in the MLD. This is in line with the general experience where most Basotho send their children to schools in South Africa (the MLD of choice). Students have the same attitude to medical services.

The usual "stick" factors that might deter someone from leaving are much less powerful in the case of Basotho students, partly because their intended destination is so close and well-known to them already. On the other hand, getting legal papers to work in South Africa has not been easy for anyone since 1994, Basotho included.[34] Opinion is mixed. Forty five percent say it would be easy to work in their most likely destination; 47% that it would be difficult.

Families can either facilitate or discourage migration. Nearly half of the students (47%) indicate their families would encourage them to leave Lesotho. Only a third say they would be discouraged from leaving. Regardless of family influence, the majority (70%) indicate the final decision would be made by them. Only 10% say the decision would be made by their spouses or parents.

How long would students stay away for? Would their emigration be temporary or permanent? Seventy percent say they want to leave for longer than two years. Forty three percent indicate that if they left they would stay away for longer than five years (Table 3.9). Nearly sixty percent of students have a strong desire to become permanent residents in their MLD. Nearly fifty percent say they would want to become citizens of their MLD. In sum, there is considerable interest amongst Basotho students in leaving Lesotho permanently and re-settling elsewhere. Would this prevent them maintaining linkages with home? From Table 3.10, it is clear that most would not be willing to break all ties.

Table 3.9: Intended Length of Stay in MLD		
Period of stay in MLD	%	Cumulative %
Less than 6 months	6.7	6.7
6 months to one year	5.6	12.3
1 to 2 years	14.0	26.3
2 to 5 years	22.1	48.4
More than 5 years	43.3	91.7
Don't know	7.2	98.9
No response	1.1	100.0
Total	100.0	N = 1,083

Asked how often they would want to return home, a large number (54%) say they would do so once at least once every few months. They would also be serious remitters. As many as 64% say they would send money home once a month. Very few indicated that they would never remit.

Table 3.10: Willingness to Cut Ties with Lesotho				
Response (%)	Give up home in Lesotho	Take all possessions out of Lesotho	Take all assets out of Lesotho	Give up citizen-ship of Lesotho
Very Willing	12.9	7.0	7.9	9.8
Willing	15.2	10.6	8.1	8.6
Unwilling	33.7	36.5	33.9	23.0
Very Unwilling	35.6	42.0	45.7	52.6
Don't know	2.6	3.9	4.4	6.0
Total	100.0	100.0	100.0	100.0
	N = 1,146	N = 1,131	N = 1,126	N = 1,106

GOVERNMENT POLICIES

What might government do to address the impending skills loss crisis? How would students respond to various possible policy measures to encourage or require them to stay in the country? More than half (54%) think it would be justified to require citizens to complete some form of national/public service before enrolling at institutions of higher learning (Table 3.11). An even larger proportion (71%) think that it would be justified to require citizens who have received government bursaries for education to complete some form of national service. There is also a general consensus that it would be justifiable to require citizens to work in the country for several years after completion of their education.

Table 3.12 suggests that changes in policy would not make a difference to the likelihood of emigration. Most (85%) think that enacting legislation which will make it more difficult for students to migrate would not discourage people from leaving Lesotho. In sum, the usual retention strategies would make very little difference if implemented in Lesotho.

CONCLUSION

Clearly, a large number of students are ready and willing to leave Lesotho on graduation. Given the fact that most students are funded out of the public purse, this is a reason for grave concern. The Lesotho government invests in training and South Africa is the primary beneficiary. Without major economic growth in Lesotho, the brain drain is probably unstoppable. The best

Table 3.11: Student Opinion About Lesotho Government Policies

	Response (%)					
	Completely Justified	Justified	Neither	Unjustified	Completely Unjustified	Don't know
Require citizens to complete some form of national/public service before enrolling at institutions of higher learning	26.6	27.3	4.8	24.2	9.4	7.6
Require citizens who have received government bursaries for education to complete some form of national service	37.4	33.4	6.7	13.7	5.5	3.4
Require citizens to work in Lesotho for several years after completion of their education	33.6	25.0	6.5	19.3	13.8	1.8

Table 3.12: Student Responses to Possible Restrictions

Probability of Emigration if Government:	Much more likely (%)	More likely (%)	No difference (%)	Less likely (%)	Much less likely (%)	Don't know (%)
Took steps to make it more difficult to emigrate	12.4	15.2	34.7	16.3	10.0	11.4
Required people leaving professional schools to do one year national service in their area of expertise	11.5	19.9	34.9	15.0	9.3	9.5
Allowed people to hold only one passport	11.5	14.8	37.3	14.5	12.6	9.4
Increased fees for emigration documents	9.7	11.6	37.3	16.4	14.2	10.9

that can be hoped for is that the new Basotho migrants will remit as regularly and as voluminously as the mine migrants of previous generations (many of whom would have been their own relatives). Lesotho government policies have to adapt to the new migration reality.

Chapter 4

The Potential Brain Drain from Swaziland

Hamilton Simelane

INTRODUCTION

Swaziland, like Lesotho, has a long history of circulatory labour migration with South Africa.[35] Between 1911 and 1985, the number of Swazi migrants in South Africa remained remarkably stable over time. The 1929 South African Census, for example, recorded 29,177 Swaziland-born people in the country. The equivalent figure sixty years later, in 1985, was 30,772.[36] For decades, migrants were primarily unskilled and semi-skilled workers in the mines, farms and households of white South Africa. More recently, and particularly since the collapse of apartheid, skilled Swazis have found it much easier to move and live and work in South Africa.[37] In 2001, the number of Swaziland-born people in South Africa had increased to 34,471.[38] Many of these individuals are part of a new wave of migration to South Africa of teachers, nurses, civil servants and academics.

The numbers involved are not known with any certainty but they will almost certainly grow in the future. As the Swazi economy stumbles and the political problems increase, so too do the attractions of moving to South Africa. In addition, new South African immigration legislation will make it much easier for skilled Swazis to migrate legally to South Africa in the future.

One index of whether the brain trickle is likely to escalate into a full-fledged brain drain in the future lies in the heads of the next generation of skilled Swazis. With that in mind, the PSBS was implemented in Swaziland to try and get a better reading of whether Swazi students still feel that their own country offers them a future or whether they, like students in other parts of the region, are also eyeing the possibility of moving to greener pastures in South Africa and elsewhere.

STUDENT PROFILE IN SWAZILAND

This chapter is based on the findings of a survey of 1,197 final year college and university students. Some 53% of the sample were pursuing certificate and diploma programmes while 36% were enrolled for Bachelor's degrees. A random sample of students some years ago in Swaziland would have yielded a predominantly male population. Today, that imbalance has been largely rectified. Of the students interviewed in this project, 48.5% were female. The vast majority (87.3%) of the students were single, with only one in ten married. Half the students say that they have no dependents. Family obligations are therefore unlikely to create barriers to movement. A third of the students (36%) identify themselves as of middle-class background, with the remainder "lower class" (34%) or working class (26%). The high percentage of students from poorer backgrounds speaks well of the accessibility of education in Swaziland. The absolute number of middle-class students in tertiary education is probably much higher since many from the middle-class actually leave the country to study.

Table 4.1: Sources of Student Support		
Form of Support	No.	%
Government scholarship (no payback required)	91	8.8
Government bursary (some payback required)	767	74.4
University scholarship (no payback required)	5	0.5
University bursary (some payback required)	10	1.0
Technicon scholarship (no payback required)	1	0.1
Technicon bursary (some payback required)	4	0.4
Personal / family funds	160	15.5
Private scholarship	28	2.7
Bank / study loan	6	0.6
Other	8	0.8
Don't know	5	0.5
Totals	1031	100.0

Government is heavily involved in student support in Swaziland with over 80% on state bursaries (Table 4.1). Institutional scholarships and bursaries are all but non-existent. Only 15.5% of students draw on personal or family funds.

The strength of Swaziland's migration ties with South Africa are reflected in the students' own life experience. Very few (less than 5%) have ever travelled to Europe, North America or Asia. On the other hand, only 10% have never been to South Africa (Table 4.2). Nearly 20% go to South Africa at least once a month and over 70% at least once a year. Most of their travels to South Africa to date have been non work-related. When they go there after graduation to look for employment, they will not be doing so as complete novices. Swazis know South Africa well and it is the most obvious place to go when leaving home.

Just over 40% of the students have immediate family members who have already emigrated from Swaziland, but only 10% say that most or almost all have left permanently (Table 4.3). The fact that over 50% have no family members who have left is instructive, if only because it indicates that there are still a large number of individual families in the country who have not yet been touched by the brain drain. That situation could change rapidly if this cohort of students acts on its intentions. Broadening the circle to include extended family members

Table 4.2: Frequency of Swazi Student Travel to South Africa		
	No.	%
More than once a month	115	9.7
Once a month	88	7.4
Once every few months	346	29.1
Once or twice a year	307	25.9
Once every few years	112	9.4
Just once or twice	97	8.2
Never	122	10.3
Total	1187	100.0

and friends, a slightly different picture emerges. Here only 25% of students report that no members of the extended family have left the country. Very similar figures were reported for close friends. Around 20% of students say that most or almost all of their close friends have already gone. The final category included colleagues, fellow students and co-workers; in other words, educated and trained people like themselves. Here, only 20% do not know of anyone who has left. This suggests that the brain drain of skilled Swazis is not a future possibility but an ongoing reality.

Table 4.3: Knowledge of People Who Have Left Swaziland								
	Immediate Family		Extended Family		Close Friends		Colleagues / Fellow Students / Co-workers	
	No.	%	No.	%	No.	%	No.	%
None	613	51.9	298	25.4	347	26.6	241	20.5
Just One or Two	290	24.5	245	20.9	248	21.2	167	14.2
Several	155	13.1	307	26.1	295	25.2	374	31.8
Most	54	4.6	159	13.6	147	12.6	163	13.8
Almost all	39	3.3	68	5.8	61	5.2	66	5.6
Don't know	31	2.6	97	8.3	72	6.1	166	14.1
Total	1,182	100.0	1,175	100.0	1,170	100.0	1,176	100.0

STUDENT ATTITUDES TO EMIGRATION

Swazi are often cited for a strong sense of national identity. Allegiance to the monarchy and traditional cultural practices are seen as important indicators of Swazi identity. At the same time the schism between the traditional and the modern has widened in Swaziland in recent years. The University campus has been a recurrent site of anti-government and anti-royal opposition and protest. The question then is to what extent students still hold a strong sense of Swazi identity in a nation undergoing unprecedented, though largely hidden, stress and conflict. The fact that so many students are from rural backgrounds, where traditional powers and mores are still strong, might reasonably be expected to influence the answer to this question.

Interestingly, about 70% of the students say they are proud to be called Swazi while only 14% say they are not. Asked whether being a citizen of Swaziland is an important part of how they see themselves, 60% answered positively while 18% responded negatively and 18% were undecided. These numbers seem fairly unequivocal yet it is worth noting, in passing, that the degree of identification is weaker than in countries such as Lesotho or Botswana where the percentage of "proud" students is much higher. Like students in Botswana and Lesotho, Swazis are also idealistic. An overwhelming 85% say they feel it is their duty to contribute their skills and talents to the country and that they also have a definite contribution to make in the development of Swaziland. This would certainly seem to indicate that given the right conditions and environment, Swazi students would prefer to remain in Swaziland and contribute their skills to the growth and development of their country.

Economic conditions at both the personal and national levels can play an important role in influencing decisions about migration. At the personal level, economic conditions can make the process of self-reproduction extremely difficult, making the potential for out-migration high. Three quarters of Swazi students express dissatisfaction with their current economic situation. However, dissatisfaction has nothing obvious to do with socio-economic background. In other words, those who are satisfied are not necessarily middle-class and not all those from poorer backgrounds are dissatisfied. Students worldwide are notoriously, and rightly, dissatisfied with their economic circumstances. Swazi students, however, are also extremely negative about the performance of the national economy with a dissatisfaction rate of 87% (and approval rate of only 3%).

What of the future? The majority of students (66%) expect their personal fortunes to have improved five years hence. However, 77% feel that the national economic situation will be worse. Perhaps this apparent contradiction is simply the opinion of the classic "impoverished" student or perhaps the students are thinking that their own fortunes are not necessarily tied to those of the national economy. Swaziland will be worse off economically in five years time but this will not affect them personally because they will be seeking their fortunes elsewhere. This hypothesis tends to be born out by evidence from the survey.

Interestingly, male students were more optimistic than females about their personal economic future. The higher negative response from females may be a reflection of the fact that students are perfectly aware that Swazi women continue to bear the brunt of poverty in Swaziland and find it more difficult to access jobs than men. It could also be a function of the fact that they see themselves as less mobile than men, although this is not confirmed in the survey as a whole.

The general gloom about the national economy and its prospects is echoed in responses to questions about what this would mean for them personally. Over 80% feel that the cost of living will get worse, for example. There is a significant difference here between rural and urban responses, with rural dwellers more pessimistic. Eighty percent feel that their ability to find the job they want will decline over the next 5 years. Only 12% and 25% respectively feel that job security and opportunities for professional advancement will improve. There is a little more optimism about income with 31% feeling that income levels will improve over the next five years. On the other hand, only 6% feel that income tax will be better in the future. On most of these measures, females were more pessimistic than males.

Swaziland is in the grip of a devastating HIV/AIDS epidemic which is cutting a swath through the education and health sectors.[39] Both sectors are also feeling the pinch of the brain drain to South Africa. Unsurprisingly, therefore, Swazi students are not at all optimistic about future service in these two sectors. Only 31% feel that medical services will improve in the next five years (46% think they will deteriorate). Similarly with schools, 35% think the situation will improve, 40% that it will get worse. Students are also not enamoured with the safety and security situation in Swaziland with over 60% thinking that the threat to personal and family security will increase. Similar numbers (63%) have no confidence in Swaziland as a place to secure their children's future.

If students perceive that conditions at home, however bad, are no better than in other countries, they will have little interest in moving. But Swazi students in overwhelming numbers do believe that things are better in at least some parts of the world than in Swaziland. For example, the majority feel that they would be better off in Europe (80%), North America (77%), Australia/New Zealand (71%) and Asia (56%). In the case of Southern African countries, South Africa (85%) and Botswana (66%) are cited as better than Swaziland. Mozambique and Zimbabwe rate poorly amongst most students. All students, male and female, arts and sciences, rural and urban, have a more positive view of South Africa than they do of any other part of the region or world.

If Swazi students had no restrictions on where they could move to if they left, most (43%) say they would opt for South Africa and Botswana. Twenty nine percent say Europe and 18% North America. Students have virtually no interest in Asia (3%) and the rest of Africa (1%). What makes South Africa and Europe and North America so attractive looking? What is it about their Most Likely Destination (MLD) that is most attractive to Swazi students? Table 4.4 shows the number of students who think a particular economic or social measure would be better in their MLD than in Swaziland. Economically, the majority of students think that Swaziland compares unfavourably with their MLD. The contrast is particularly marked in relation to income, prospects for professional advancement and ability to find the right job. On most social measures (including health), Swaziland also comes off worse. Only in the case of personal and family safety issues do slightly fewer than half of the students believe that the situation is better in their MLD. In the case of HIV/AIDS, around half think the situation is better in their MLD. The fact that so many students see South Africa as their MLD obviously affects their perception of safety issues. On the other hand, South Africa is clearly seen as superior on just about every other economic and social measure used in the survey.

Table 4.4: Comparison of Swaziland with MLD		
Better in the Most Likely Destination:	No.	(%)
Economic		
Level of Income	850	93.8
Right Job	626	70.1
Professional advancement	758	85.5
Cost of Living	528	58.1
Job Security	534	67.1
Taxation Level	413	57.1
Social		
HIV / AIDS Situation	396	50.6
Children's future	489	59.1
Children's Schooling	675	77.5
Family Safety	380	47.6
Medial Care	707	82.4
Personal Safety	398	48.9
Housing	625	75.4
Public Amenities	717	85.9

Which of these factors is likely to exercise the strongest pull on students? While it is important to recognize that any migration decision is complex and cannot be reduced to a single reason, students were asked to provide the single most important reason why they might leave. Table 4.5 shows that economic/employment considerations are actually far more important than social (including health) differences when it comes to migration decisions. Less than 5% mentioned social factors as a primary reason for leaving. Even the HIV/AIDS epidemic is not, in itself, considered to be a strong reason for going. Income and an inability to find the "right" job in Swaziland are easily the most important reasons for leaving. Other factors – cost of living, job security and taxes – are much less significant.

Table 4.5: Most Important Reason for Leaving Swaziland		
	No.	%
Economic		
Level of Income	279	33.4
Right Job	256	30.7
Professional Advancement	124	14.9
Cost of Living	84	10.0
Job Security	24	2.8
Taxation Level	13	1.5
Social		
HIV AIDS Situation	15	1.7
Children's future	9	1.1
Children's Schooling	7	0.9
Family Safety	6	0.8
Medical Care	6	0.8
Personal Safety	5	0.6
Housing	4	0.5
Public Amenities	1	0.1
Total	833	100.0

While there are many reasons why people might leave, it usually involves some calculation and comparison of conditions here and conditions there. As we have seen, economic rather than social factors are paramount in the thinking of Swazis. On the other hand, there are usually a host of "stick" factors making an early exit less likely. These often relate to social issues such as family obligations and preferences. Other SAMP research has shown that gender, cross-cutting with race and occupation, is also an important determinant of emigration potential amongst seasoned professionals.[40] Because many Swazi are very family-oriented it is important to see how much decision-making autonomy students feel they have and whether their families think it would be a good idea for them to leave.

Swazi families are perhaps not quite as encouraging of emigration as Basotho families but only 30% of students say that they would be discouraged from leaving. More (39%) say that their departure would be encouraged. Contrary to expectations, more women (249) than men (212) say their families would encourage them to leave. Historically, Swazi families have tended to discourage female migration using a variety of reasons to justify their position. That is why in most migration streams from Swaziland in the past there have been limited numbers of women.[41] But these are different times. Education, and the fact that some young women are now breadwinners for their families, have engendered a new attitude. Families have been forced to accept that because of the skills they now possess, daughters can migrate with the same intensity and positive impacts as sons. Regardless of whether the family puts up obstacles or encourages emigration, the majority of students (67%) say the decision is up to them. Only 18% say their parents would decide for them. Times have clearly changed.

The pre-conditions for an accelerating brain drain appear to be in place. Swazi students are prepped to look beyond the borders of the country, perhaps unlike any other moment in Swazi history. And the people who leave will be those whose skills and dedication is most needed at home. What, then, are the emigration intentions of today's student at the university and technical colleges? The majority of students have certainly thought about leaving. But how likely is it that they will actually do so? As many as 62% say it is likely (33%) or very likely (28%) that they will leave for a period of more than two years (Table 4.6).

Table 4.6: Likelihood of Leaving Swaziland for More than Two Years		
	No.	%
Very likely	301	28.4
Likely	351	33.1
Unlikely	202	19.1
Very unlikely	104	9.9
Do not know	101	9.5
Total	1060	100.0

Confirming not only the high rate of likely departure but the penchant for an extended period away, only 20% say they would want to stay in their MLD for less than two years (Table 4.7). A massive 44% say they would want to stay away for more than five years. Whether they will all actually do so is, of course, debatable but it is clear that the potential move to South Africa is not seen as a short-term palliative but a longer-term commitment.

Table 4.7: Desired Length of Stay in MLD		
	No.	%
Less than 6 months	30	2.6
6 months to one year	59	5.0
1 to 2 years	141	12.0
2 to 5 years	313	26.6
More than 5 years	514	43.7
Do not know	118	10.0
Total	1176	100.0

Moving to South Africa does not mean cutting ties with Swaziland. On the contrary, once relocated only 4% say they would never return. Twenty percent would return at least once a month and over 80% would return at least once a year. Less than two percent say they would never send money home. Seventy six percent say they would remit at lease once a month and a further 16% "a few times a year." The loss of newly minted skills is a serious problem, partially offset by the fact that so many Swazi would remit funds home once they had left.

The desire to retain strong backward linkages after departure is confirmed by other measures. Just 23% say that they have a strong wish to become permanent residents of another country. However, only 22% say they have no desire suggesting that the question remains an open one for the majority. Similarly, 24% have a strong desire to become citizens of another country and 24% have no desire at all. On the other hand, 70% have no desire to be buried in another country, suggesting that eventual return to Swaziland is anticipated. The attachment to Swaziland is further demonstrated by a reluctance to give up a home in Swaziland (75% unwilling) and Swazi citizenship (73% unwilling).

GOVERNMENT POLICIES

The Swaziland government has shown little public concern about the brain drain to South Africa to date. If and when it does, it is likely to consider the same set of measures adopted by other governments faced with a crippling skills loss. How would Swazi students respond to such measures? First, 40% say that government steps to make emigration difficult would have no impact on their decision to move from Swaziland. Twenty one percent say it would make them more likely to emigrate and 19% that it would make them less likely. In other words, the majority of Swazi students feel that government interventions would not deter or inhibit them from leaving.

On specific measures that government might take, 47% are opposed and 38% in favour of some form of national/public service before enrolling at institutions of higher learning. Bonding is one policy option pursued by many African governments. Here, nationals are required to work in the country for a specified number of years after completion of their training. About 50% of Swazi students disagree with bonding, with 36% saying it would be justified. Half of the respondents feel that out-migration would be reduced if positive measures were introduced by government to encourage the return of qualified professionals, while 33% feel that such measures would not change the situation. Swazi students also feel that measures to discourage destination countries from employing emigrants from Swaziland will not reduce emigration. Economic policies were seen as having a much greater potential impact than political interventions. Some 83% feel that only greater local economic development would reduce out-migration.

Chapter 5

The Potential Brain Drain from Namibia

Selma Nangulah

INTRODUCTION

P rior to independence in 1990, few institutions provided tertiary education for Namibians.[42] The apartheid regime had little interest in educating the mass of the Namibian population beyond the most rudimentary levels. It is only over the last decade that the Namibian government has invested resources to provide tertiary educational opportunities for citizens in order to meet the skills requirements of the public and private sector. If many of these newly trained professionals now decide to leave Namibia, it could create a serious problem for the country.

Namibia does not have the long and entrenched history of mass migration to South Africa that characterizes the other countries studied in this publication. A previous SAMP study in 1998 found few Namibians who wanted to emigrate to South Africa.[43] However, there have been recent media reports in Namibia of growing numbers of Namibian health professionals moving to developed countries.[44] This at least suggests that Namibia is coming under the same sorts of pressure as other countries in SADC to yield up its professionals to the regional and global skills market. One of the more obvious and convenient places to go would be South Africa. No research has been conducted on the propensity of skilled Namibians to leave for South Africa. This study is the first attempt to investigate the likelihood of brain drain depletion of Namibia's future skills base.

STUDENT PROFILE IN NAMIBIA

T he PSBS study was carried out among students from 10 tertiary educational institutions in Namibia. A total of 1,200 students were interviewed. Eighty percent of the interviews were conducted in Windhoek, the capital city. There were slightly more male (52%) than female students (48%) and the majority (63%) were young (23 years or less). As many as 91% of the students were single. Almost half (47%) were from the rural communal areas, while 25% came from small towns. Very few came from a city (14%), large town (10%) or the commercial farming areas (5%). Around one in ten saw themselves as upper middle to upper class (9%). Twenty eight percent said they were middle class and the remainder working-class and "lower-class."

Most language groups were represented at about the same ratio as in the national population (Figure 5.1). Oshiwambo-speaking students (at 46%) made up the majority of respondents, followed by Lozi speakers (11%) and Damara/Nama (10%). Otjiherero and Rukwangali-speaking students were 7% and 9%, respectively; Afrikaans speakers made up 8% and English speakers 4%.

Figure 5.1: The home language breakdown of respondents

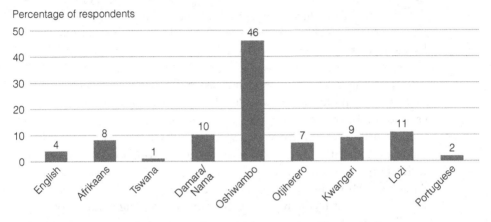

The students were drawn from ten separate institutions with the majority (66.7%) from the University of Namibia (Table 5.1). They represented a broad cross-section of faculties and disciplines from education (40%), technical courses (22%), science (13%), arts/social sciences/humanities (7%) and commerce and business (7%). The sample also included 44 students in medicine/pharmacy. Most students were enrolled full-time. Forty four percent were studying for Bachelor's degrees and 56% for certificates or diplomas. Only Namibian citizens and students with permanent residence were interviewed.

Table 5.1: Tertiary Institutions Sampled		
Institution	No.	%
University of Namibia	801	66.7
Polytechnic of Namibia	207	17.2
Ongwediva College of Education	64	5.3
Windhoek College of Education	37	3.1
Rundu College of Education	27	2.3
Rundu Vocational Training Centre	20	1.6
Windhoek Vocational Training Centre	18	1.5
Valombola Vocational Training Centre	14	1.2
Ogongo Agricultural College	5	0.5
Neudamm Agricultural College	6	0.5
Total	1199	100

Table 5.2: Sample by Institution/Programme		
Faculty	No.	%
University: Faculty of Engineering	9	0.8
University: Faculty of Medicine/Pharmacy	44	3.7
University: Faculty of Science	156	13
University: Faculty of Arts/Social Science and Humanities	87	7.3
University: Faculty of Law	17	1.4
University: Faculty of Commerce/Business	78	6.5
University: Faculty of Computer Science/IT	11	0.9
University: Faculty of Agriculture	36	3
University: Other	2	0.2
University: Faculty of Education	354	29.6
Technical College/Technicon: Technical Subjects	129	10.8
Technical College/Technicon: Commerce/Administration	98	8.2
Technical College/Technicon: IT/Computers	9	0.7
Technical College/Technicon: Other	23	1.9
Teacher Training College	129	10.7
Agricultural Training College	11	0.9
Total	1,184	100

Financial support for tertiary education in Namibia comes from a variety of sources. 40% of students are on government bursaries or scholarships (with 33% requiring some form of payback) (Table 5.3).

Table 5.3: Sources of Student Financial Support in Namibia		
Sources of support for study training	No.	%
Government scholarship (no payback required)	70	5.3
Government bursary (some payback required)	438	32.7
University scholarship (no payback required)	9	0.7
University bursary (some payback required)	17	1.2
Technicon scholarship (no payback required)	1	0.1
Technicon bursary (some payback required)	7	0.5
Personal family funds	459	34.3
Private scholarship	127	9.5
Bank/study loan	200	14.9
Other sources	7	0.6
Don't know	4	0.3
Total	1339*	100
*N >1,200 as some students have more than one source of funding		

Other significant sources of funding include private monies (34% of students), bank loans (15%) and private scholarships (10%). About a third of the students say they are required to work in the public sector as a form of payback, while 11% are required to work for the private sector.

A strong sense of national pride is reported by the students who show very positive attitudes towards (a) being Namibian, (b) being citizens, and (c) wanting their children to think of themselves as Namibians. Students from rural backgrounds are marginally more positive than those of urban origin. Students exhibit a strong desire to help build Namibia (94% in favour), and believe it their duty to contribute their talents and skills to the growth of their country (93%). Most believe that they have a role to play in the future of their country. A majority (68%) feel that they have an "important role" to play personally, while 24% indicate that they have "some role" to play

Namibian students are far less negative about their personal and national economic circumstances than those from the other countries considered here. Only 27% are dissatisfied with their own circumstances and 22% with national economic conditions. They are also far more optimistic about the future. Nearly 80% of the students believe that their economic condition and that of the country will improve over the next five years.

However, there are mixed feelings among students about particular economic indicators (Table 5.4). About the same number think that the cost of living will improve and that it will get worse. They are similarly divided about whether they can get the job they want. More think that their earnings will be significantly greater and that job security will improve. They would, however, expect to be paying higher taxes, presumably to pay for what they predict as an improvement in healthcare, schooling and public amenities. Again, students from rural backgrounds are more optimistic about the future than those from urban backgrounds.

Students were asked to compare Namibia with other countries. South Africa is the only country in Southern Africa which the majority of students (71%) think is "better off" than Namibia. South Africa compares favourably with Europe and North America in the eyes of Namibian students (Table 5.5). A number of countries are seen as no better or worse off than Namibia. Only in the case of Zimbabwe, however, do a clear majority of students consider themselves to be better off in Namibia.

As noted above, Namibia does not have a strong tradition of emigration. This is reflected in the fact that, in contrast to Lesotho and Swaziland for example, most students are not aware of many people who have left the country permanently (Table 5.6). However, the more the

Table 5.4: Expectations about the Future in Namibia				
Response Category	Better (%)	About the same (%)	Worse (%)	Don't know (%)
Cost of living	41	13	43	2
Ability to find the job I want	36	21	40	3
Prospects for professional advancement	52	22	15	12
HIV/AIDS situation	20	7	69	3
The security of your job	39	28	20	13
Your level of income	58	20	12	10
Ability to find the house you want to live in	46	20	28	7
Ability to find a good school for your children	56	17	21	5
Ability to find medical services for your family and children	59	21	17	5
A level of fair taxation	22	26	37	15
Your personal safety	40	24	29	6
Your family's safety	42	25	27	6
The future of your children in Namibia	54	18	17	11
Quality upkeep of public amenities (e.g. Parks, beaches, toilets etc.)	52	21	21	6
Availability of affordable quality products	44	20	28	8
Customer service	52	23	15	9

sphere of questioning is expanded from the immediate family, the higher the number of people known to have left the country.

Namibian students also have very limited personal travel experience. Although there has been very little travel among students outside Namibia, some 41% have traveled to countries within Southern Africa, most only occasionally. Fewer students have traveled to other parts of the world.

Given their high levels of commitment to their country, relative satisfaction with life and future prospects, and the fact that they have limited personal or vicarious exposure to life outside Namibia, it would be surprising to find that many Namibian students are interested in leaving after graduation. However, this is far from the case.

A total of 29% have given a great deal of consideration to leaving and a further 40% have given it some consideration. Women, urban-

Table 5.5: Comparison Between Namibia and Other Countries

Countries	Much Better (%)	Better (%)	About the same (%)	Worse (%)	Much worse (%)	Don't know (%)
Botswana	12	26	34	13	4	11
Lesotho	5	22	34	18	4	18
Mozambique	2	15	32	27	8	17
Swaziland	7	22	34	16	5	16
Zimbabwe	3	12	23	28	24	10
South Africa	30	41	17	5	2	6
Angola	9	19	20	25	15	11
Malawi	3	16	27	27	7	20
Zambia	4	14	26	27	15	14
East Africa	4	17	24	19	11	25
West Africa	5	20	24	19	9	23
Central Africa	4	17	26	21	10	23
North Africa	7	23	22	18	7	23
Europe	44	32	8	5	3	9
North America	41	31	8	6	3	10
Australia / New Zealand	38	31	11	5	2	14
Asia/China	23	27	16	10	6	18

Table 5.6: Knowledge of People Who Have Left Namibia

No. of people	Immediate family (%)	Extended family (%)	Close friends (%)	Fellow students / colleagues / co-workers (%)
None	69	51	48	39
One – Two	18	21	22	18
Several	7	13	17	19
Most	2	5	5	11
Almost all	4	1	3	4

based students, and those from more affluent families have given more consideration to moving. Only 27% report that they have never thought of moving at all.

Thinking about moving is not the same thing as thinking it is likely to happen. Nearly thirty percent of the students think it is likely or very likely that they will be gone within six months of graduation. The proportion rises to 47% within two years and 58% within five years. What this seems to confirm is that there is a sizable minority (perhaps a third) in Namibia who are interested in leaving and think it likely that they will do so. Over time, this number may grow.

Table 5.7: Likelihood of Leaving Namibia After Graduation						
Response	Within Six months		Within Two years		Within Five years	
	No.	%	No.	%	No.	%
Very likely	127	11	162	14	310	27
Likely	199	17	382	33	357	31
Unlikely	293	26	288	25	163	14
Very unlikely	374	33	195	17	170	15
Do not know	152	13	119	10	148	13
Totals	1,145	100	1,146	100	1,148	100

Only a few students (8%) say they have already applied for a work permit, with 15% of the students in the process of applying. The rest (77%) say that they have not applied for work permits elsewhere. Only a handful of students say that have applied for a permanent resident permit (4%) or citizenship (4%) in another country.

Although 65 countries are mentioned as most likely destinations by students, South Africa (26%), the USA (13%) and the UK (12%) are the most popular. A comparison between Namibia and the MLD should shed some light on why students think they will probably leave the country. How does Namibia fare in such comparisons? On most economic and social issues, students are fairly evenly split (Table 5.8), which suggests that only the sizable minority thinks that the grass is greener on the other side.

Asked more directly for the most important reason why they would leave, no single reason stands out. Prospects for professional advancement are mentioned by 20% as the most important reason, while cost of living, level of income and finding a desirable job are all cited by approximately 15% of the students. There are few unequivocal clues here to explain the strong desire to leave amongst the sizable minority.

One possible alternative, non-economic explanation is that students are being encouraged by their families to leave the country. Here there is some supporting evidence. As many as 36% of the students are being encouraged by their families to leave (with only 27% being actively discouraged). Another possible, non-economic influence is the HIV/AIDS epidemic. Almost half of the students indicated that the HIV/AIDS rate in Namibia might influence their decision to move. Only 27% said it would have no influence.

What is striking is that even the members of the sizable minority see

Table 5.8: Comparison of Namibia with the MLD

Comparisons	Much better in Namibia		Better in Namibia		About the same		Better in MLD		Much better in MLD		Do not know	
	No.	%	No.	%	No.	%	No.	%	No.	%	No.	%
Cost of living	236	20	284	24	172	15	266	23	154	13	63	5
Ability to find job I want	133	12	290	25	218	20	282	24	148	13	88	8
Prospects for professional advancement	67	6	184	16	187	16	325	28	268	23	121	11
HIV/AIDS situation	41	4	117	10	306	26	243	21	243	21	214	18
Security of your job	82	7	287	25	216	19	256	22	168	15	147	13
Your level of income	59	5	143	13	124	11	388	34	333	29	92	8
Ability to find a house you want	134	12	291	25	212	18	293	25	261	22	105	9
Ability to find good school for your children	91	8	195	17	198	17	346	30	253	22	85	7
Ability to find medical services for your family	82	7	229	20	198	17	293	25	261	22	105	9
A level of fair taxation	71	6	245	21	277	24	191	16	115	10	264	23
Your personal safety	154	13	294	26	233	20	210	18	161	14	100	9
Your family's safety	161	14	327	28	203	18	202	18	144	13	118	10
The future of your children in Namibia	148	13	293	25	203	18	190	16	210	18	117	10
Quality upkeep of public amenities	58	5	156	13	199	17	311	27	334	29	116	10
Availability of affordable quality products	67	6	150	13	172	15	361	31	302	26	117	10
Customer service	72	6	143	12	204	17	311	27	269	23	175	15

emigration as a temporary rather than permanent phenomenon. Very few students (16%) are willing to stay for less than a year in their MLD, but rather want to stay for 1 – 2 years (26%), 2 – 5 years (26%) or more than 5 years (22%). Once they have moved to their MLD, students indicate that they are likely to return home yearly (40%), every few months (24%) or every few years (15%). However, most students indicate that they are not ready to become permanent residents or citizens in their MLD. Retiring or being buried there is out of the question. Most would also retain strong linkages with home, being unwilling to give up their Namibian homes, remove all their assets and possessions from Namibia or give up Namibian citizenship (Table 5.9).

Table 5.9: Ongoing Links with Namibia										
	Very Willing		Willing		Very Unwilling		Unwilling		Don't know	
	No.	%	No.	%	No.	%	No.	%	No.	%
Give up your home in Namibia	83	7	175	15	444	38	423	36	57	5
Take all your possessions out of Namibia	47	4	101	9	429	36	548	47	51	4
Take all your assets out of Namibia	44	4	108	9	375	32	593	51	53	5
Give up citizenship in Namibia	46	4	85	7	297	25	683	58	61	5

GOVERNMENT POLICIES

There are mixed feelings among students about national service in Namibia. Around half feel that the Namibian government would be justified in requiring that citizens complete some form of national or public service before enrolling at institutions of higher learning. A third disagree. More (70%) agree that citizens who have received government bursaries should complete some form of national or public service or be required to work in the country for several years after completion of their studies. Students from rural backgrounds are generally more supportive of these measures than those from urban areas.

Most students feel that changes in government policy to make emigration more difficult will not stop nationals from moving away from home (Table 5.10). Thirty percent feel it would make no difference and 27% that it would make people more inclined to leave. However, there is more support for the government to require people leaving professional schools to do one year of national service in their area of expertise and for the government to allow people to hold only one passport.

Table 5.10: Responses to Possible Restrictions on Emigration

Probability of emigration if government:	Much more likely (%)	More likely (%)	No difference (%)	Less likely (%)	Much less likely (%)	Don't know (%)
Took steps to make it more difficult to emigrate	9	18	31	19	9	14
Required people leaving professional schools to do one year national service in their area of expertise	11	23	27	19	7	13
Allowed people to hold only one passport	11	20	32	15	9	13
Increased fees for emigration	8	14	33	16	16	14

On the other hand, there is some support for direct government intervention (presumably not from the sizable minority) (Table 5.11). For example, 45% think the government should enact legislation to

Table 5.11: Level of Support for Government Policy on Emigration

Category	Yes (%)	No (%)	Don't know (%)
Encourage economic development, which will discourage people from leaving	77	12	11
Enact legislation, which will make it more difficult for students to migrate	45	36	19
Institute measures, which encourage the return of qualified professionals abroad	60	22	18
Forging links with destination countries of emigrants from Namibia to discourage them from employing emigrants from emigrants from Namibia	42	35	23
Prohibit emigration	48	36	16
None (no steps to reduce emigration)	18	30	52
Other steps	8	18	74

make it more difficult for students to leave on graduation and 48% that the government should simply prohibit emigration. As many as 42% feel the government should enter into agreements with other countries to discourage them from employing Namibians. Non-coercive measures also garnered support. A massive 77% feel the best way to discourage people from leaving is to promote economic development. As many as 60% feel that the government should encourage the return of qualified Namibians from abroad.

CONCLUSION

The most important finding of this study is that Namibia, despite a limited history of emigration, faces a future brain drain and its accompanying problems and challenges. There is considerable interest amongst Namibia's future professionals in leaving the country after graduation. On the other hand, not that many have so far taken active steps to leave. At this point, therefore, some of the sentiment may be wishful thinking rather than definite possibility. However, it is clear that there is a sizable minority of students who seem fairly serious about leaving (perhaps around a third). Most identified South Africa, the US and the UK as likely destinations.

All Namibian students are extremely patriotic and relatively optimistic about their country. As a result, no overwhelming reason could be identified for wanting to leave. There seems to be a combination of factors including, on the economic side, level of income, professional advancement and cost of living, and, on the non-economic, family encouragement and the HIV/AIDS epidemic.

All Namibian students have a strong feeling that they have an important role to play in the development of their country. Even members of the sizable minority feel strongly about this. It is therefore not surprising to find that students see departure from Namibia as temporary rather than permanent and few intend to sever their links with home once they had left. To attribute all of this to wanderlust or a youthful enthusiasm to see the world or, more likely, to acquire further training, might not be too short of the mark. Certainly the levels of restlessness and desire to leave are not as high amongst Namibians as they are in other countries of the region. At the same time, there are no grounds for complacency or the sizable minority could rapidly become a significant majority.

ACKNOWLEDGEMENTS

The author would like to give a word of appreciation to the individuals who made this study possible. I would like to thank Martin Shapi, Daniel Shapi, Laurencia Mutrifa, Willem Iindjembe, Mathew Haufiku, C. Ntema and A.T. Runone in assisting during the data collection process from the different tertiary institutions. I would also like to thank the positive cooperation received from the heads of departments from the different institutions. Christa Schier did the data entry and produced the tables for analysis. I would also like to thank Prof. Wade Pendleton for his support throughout the production of this report.

ENDNOTES

1   For example, L. Lowell and A. Findlay, *Migration of Highly Skilled Persons from Developing Countries: Impact and Policy Responses* (Geneva: ILO, 2001); P. Collier, A. Hoeffler and C. Pattillo, "Africa's Exodus: Capital Flight and the Brain Drain as Portfolio Decisions" *Journal of African Economies* 13(1) (2004): i15-i54; Hatton and J. Williamson, *Demographic and Economic Pressure on Emigration Out of Africa*, NBER Working Paper No 8124, Cambridge, Mass., 2001; H. Bhorat, J. B. Meyer and C. Mlatsheni, *Skilled Labour Migration from Developing Countries: Study on South and Southern Africa*, International Migration Papers No. 52, (Geneva: International Migration Programme, International Labour Office, 2002); Ted Schrecker and Ron Labonte, "Taming the Brain Drain: A Challenge for Public Health Systems in Southern Africa" *International Journal of Occupational and Environmental Health* 10(4) (2004): 409-15; Delanyo Dovlo, "The Brain Drain in Africa: An Emerging Challenge to Health Professionals Education" *Journal of Higher Education in Africa* 2(2) (2005).

2   United Nations, *Replacement Migration: Is It a Solution to Declining and Ageing Populations?* UN Population Division, New York, 2000.

3   W. Carrington and E. Detragiache, "How Big is the Brain Drain?" IMF Working Papers 98/102, 1998; M. Brown, D. Kaplan and Jean-Baptiste Meyer, "The Brain Drain: An Outline of Skilled Emigration from South Africa" In David A McDonald and Jonathan Crush (eds) *Destinations Unknown: Perspectives on the Brain Drain in Southern Africa*, (Pretoria: Africa Institute of South Africa, 2002), pp.99-112; T. Hatton and J. Williamson, "Out of Africa? Using the Past to Project Future African Demand for Emigration" *Review of International Economics* 10 (2002): 556-73; J Eastwood, R. Conroy, S. Naicker, P. West, R. Tutt and J. Plange-Rhule, "Loss of Health Professionals from Sub-Saharan Africa: The Pivotal Role of the UK" *The Lancet* 365 (2005): 1893-90; A. Hagopan, M. Thompson, M. Fordyce, K. Johnson and L. Hart, "The Migration of Physicians from Sub-Saharan Africa to the United States of America: Measures of the African Brain Drain" *Human Resources for Health* 2 (2004): 17

4   See the views of SADC professionals reported in McDonald and Crush, *Destinations Unknown.*

5   Ibid. and B. Odunsi, "An Analysis of Brain-Drain and its Impact on Manpower: Development in Nigeria" *Journal of Third World Studies* 13 (1996): 193-214

6   Robert Mattes, Jonathan Crush and Wayne Richmond, "The Brain Gain and Legal Immigration to Post-Apartheid South Africa" In McDonald and Crush, *Destinations Unknown*, pp. 139-56; Jonathan Crush, "The Global Raiders: Nationalism, Globalization and the South African Brain Drain" *Journal of International Affairs* 56 (2002): 147-72.

7 The 2001 Census (unlike the 1996 Census) also collected information on place of birth. The Census recorded 539,474 blacks born in other SADC countries and 29,880 born in the Rest of Africa. The discrepancy between foreign-born and citizenship numbers (particularly with regard to people from other SADC countries) is attributable to the naturalization of long-standing residents including immigration amnesties in the 1990s; see Jonathan Crush and Vincent Williams, eds., *The New South Africans? Immigration Amnesties and Their Aftermath* (Cape Town: Idasa, 1999); and Nicola Johnston, "The Point of No Return: Evaluating the Amnesty for Mozambican Refugees in South Africa" SAMP Migration Policy Briefs, No. 6, 2001.

8 By April 2001, South Africa had approved 17,198 African refugee applications; see Jeff Handmaker, "No Easy Walk: Advancing Refugee Protection in South Africa" *Africa Today* 48(3) (2001), p. 112.

9 Sally Peberdy, "Imagining Immigration: Inclusive Identities and Exclusive Policies in Post-1994 South Africa" *Africa Today* 48(3) (2001): 15-34.

10 Republic of South Africa (May 31, 2002). "Immigration Act, 2002". Act No. 13, 2002. *Government Gazette* Vol 443 No 23478. Cape Town.

11 Southern African Development Community, *Draft Protocol on the Facilitation of Movement of Persons*, 3rd Draft, 16 August 2005.

12 John Oucho and Jonathan Crush, "Contra Free Movement: South Africa and SADC Migration Protocols" *Africa Today* 48(3) (2001): 139-58.

13 Dan Tevera and Jonathan Crush, *The New Brain Drain from Zimbabwe*, Southern African Migration Project, Migration Policy Series No. 29, Cape Town, 2003.

14 McDonald and Crush, *Destinations Unknown*.

15 Jonathan Crush, Wade Pendleton and Daniel Tevera, *Degrees of Uncertainty: Students and the Brain Drain in Southern Africa*, Southern African Migration Project, Migration Policy Series No. 35, Cape Town, 2005, 3.

16 John Oucho, Eugene Cambell and Elizabeth Mukamaambo, *Botswana: Migration Perspectives and Prospects*, Southern African Migration Project, Migration Policy Series No. 19, Cape Town, 2000; and Eugene Campbell, "Preferences for Emigration Among Skilled Citizens in Botswana" *International Journal of Population Geography* 7(3) (2001):151-71.

17 John Gay, "Lesotho and South Africa: Time for a New Immigration Compact" In David McDonald, ed, *On Borders: Perspectives on International Migration in Southern Africa* (New York: St Martin's Press, 2000), pp. 25-45.

18 Hamilton Simelane and Jonathan Crush, *Swaziland Moves: Perceptions and Patterns of Modern Migration*, Southern African Migration Project, Migration Policy Series No. 32, Cape Town, 2004.

19 Bruce Frayne and Wade Pendleton, *Mobile Namibia: Migration Trends and Attitudes*, Southern African Migration Project, Migration Policy Series No. 27, Cape Town, 2002.

20 Botswana (1991) *National Development Plan 7, 1991-1997*. Government Printer: Gaborone. Botswana (1998) *National Development Plan 8, 1997/98-2002/03*. Government Printer: Gaborone.

21 Campbell, "Preferences for Emigration."

22 Oucho, Cambell and Mukamaambo, *Botswana: Migration Perspectives and Prospects*.

23 Ibid

24 Ibid

25 Eugene K. Campbell, "To Stay or Not to Stay: Perspectives on the Emigration Potential of Skilled Batswana", in Mcdonald, *On Borders*, pp. 139-156.

26 Macro-economic impacts of the HIV/AIDS epidemic in Botswana, *Socioeconomic Impact of HIV/AIDS in Botswana* (Gaborone: Government of Botswana, UNDP, 2000).

27 E. Campbell, "Attitudes of Botswana Citizens Toward Immigrants: Signs of Xenophobia? *International Migration*, 41(4) 2003: 71-111.

28 Colin Murray, *Families Divided* (Cambridge, 1981).

29 David Coplan, "Good for Blacks: Lesotho Migration in Post-Apartheid in South Africa" in J. Adesina and a. El-Kenz, eds., *Labour Movements and Policy Making in Africa* (Dakar: CODESRIA, 2000).

30 *Statistics South Africa – Census 2001*.

31 John Gay, "Migration Attitudes of Skilled Professionals in Lesotho", in Mcdonald and Crush, *Destinations Unknown*, pp. 181-206.

32 David Coplan and Tim Quinlan, "A Chief by the People: Nation versus State in Lesotho" *Africa* 67(1) (1997): 46-102; David Coplan, "Locations of nation: Mobility and Locality in the cultural Economy of Lesotho" in K. Follberg-Stolberg et al, eds., *Dissociation and Appropriation* (Berlin: Zentrum Modener Orient, 1999), pp. 235-54; and David Coplan, "A River Runs Through it: The Meaning of the Lesotho-Free State Border", *African Affairs* 100 (2001): 81-116.

33 John Gay, "Lesotho and South Africa: Time for a New Immigration Compact" in Mcdonald, *On Borders*, pp. 25-45; and David Mcdonald et al, "Guess Who's Coming to Dinner: Migration from Lesotho, Mozambique and Zimbabwe to South Africa" *International Migration Review* 34(3) (2000), pp. 813-41.

34 Jonathan Crush and David Mcdonald, "Evaluating South African Immigration Policy After Apartheid" *Africa Today* 48(3) (2001): 1-13.

35 Jonathan Crush. *The Struggle for Swaziland Labour 1890-1920* (Kingston and Montreal: McGill-Queen's Press 1987) and Hamilton Simelane, *Colonialism and Economic Change in Swaziland, 1940-1960* (Manzini: Jan, 2003).

36 Jonathan Crush, "Migrations Past: An Historical Overview of Cross-Border Movement in Southern Africa" In Mcdonald, *On Borders*, pp. 12-24.

37 C. Rogerson, *International Migration: Immigrant Entrepreneurs and South*

Africa's Small Enterprise Economy, SAMP Policy Series No. 3, 1997.

38 Statistics South Africa - Census 2001.

39 Sabelo Gumedze, HIV/AIDS and Human Rights in Swaziland (Pretoria: Centre for the Study of AIDS, 2004).

40 Belinda Dodson, Women in the Brain Drain: Gender and Skilled Migration from South Africa, in Mcdonald, On Borders, pp. 47-72.

41 Miranda Miles, Missing Women: A Study of Swazi Female Migration to the Witwatersrand, 1920-1970, MA Thesis, Queen's University, Kingston, 1991.

42 Elizabeth Amukugo, Education and Politics in Namibia: Past Trends and Future Prospects (Windhoek: Gamsberg Macmillan, 1995).

43 Bruce Frayne and Wade Pendleton, Mobile Namibia: Migration Trends and Attitudes, SAMP Migration Policy Series No. 27, 2002.

44 "Brain drain – calls for compensation", New Era, Feb 25, 2005

MIGRATION POLICY SERIES

1. *Covert Operations: Clandestine Migration, Temporary Work and Immigration Policy in South Africa* (1997) ISBN 1-874864-51-9
2. *Riding the Tiger: Lesotho Miners and Permanent Residence in South Africa* (1997) ISBN 1-874864-52-7
3. *International Migration, Immigrant Entrepreneurs and South Africa's Small Enterprise Economy* (1997) ISBN 1-874864-62-4
4. *Silenced by Nation Building: African Immigrants and Language Policy in the New South Africa* (1998) ISBN 1-874864-64-0
5. *Left Out in the Cold? Housing and Immigration in the New South Africa* (1998) ISBN 1-874864-68-3
6. *Trading Places: Cross-Border Traders and the South African Informal Sector* (1998) ISBN 1-874864-71-3
7. *Challenging Xenophobia: Myth and Realities about Cross-Border Migration in Southern Africa* (1998) ISBN 1-874864-70-5
8. *Sons of Mozambique: Mozambican Miners and Post-Apartheid South Africa* (1998) ISBN 1-874864-78-0
9. *Women on the Move: Gender and Cross-Border Migration to South Africa* (1998) ISBN 1-874864-82-9.
10. *Namibians on South Africa: Attitudes Towards Cross-Border Migration and Immigration Policy* (1998) ISBN 1-874864-84-5.
11. *Building Skills: Cross-Border Migrants and the South African Construction Industry* (1999) ISBN 1-874864-84-5
12. *Immigration & Education: International Students at South African Universities and Technikons* (1999) ISBN 1-874864-89-6
13. *The Lives and Times of African Immigrants in Post-Apartheid South Africa* (1999) ISBN 1-874864-91-8
14. *Still Waiting for the Barbarians: South African Attitudes to Immigrants and Immigration* (1999) ISBN 1-874864-91-8
15. *Undermining Labour: Migrancy and Sub-contracting in the South African Gold Mining Industry* (1999) ISBN 1-874864-91-8
16. *Borderline Farming: Foreign Migrants in South African Commercial Agriculture* (2000) ISBN 1-874864-97-7
17. *Writing Xenophobia: Immigration and the Press in Post-Apartheid South Africa* (2000) ISBN 1-919798-01-3
18. *Losing Our Minds: Skills Migration and the South African Brain Drain* (2000) ISBN 1-919798-03-x
19. *Botswana: Migration Perspectives and Prospects* (2000) ISBN 1-919798-04-8
20. *The Brain Gain: Skilled Migrants and Immigration Policy in Post-Apartheid South Africa* (2000) ISBN 1-919798-14-5
21. *Cross-Border Raiding and Community Conflict in the Lesotho-South African Border Zone* (2001) ISBN 1-919798-16-1

22. *Immigration, Xenophobia and Human Rights in South Africa* (2001) ISBN 1-919798-30-7
23. *Gender and the Brain Drain from South Africa* (2001) ISBN 1-919798-35-8
24. *Spaces of Vulnerability: Migration and HIV/AIDS in South Africa* (2002) ISBN 1-919798-38-2
25. *Zimbabweans Who Move: Perspectives on International Migration in Zimbabwe* (2002) ISBN 1-919798-40-4
26. *The Border Within: The Future of the Lesotho-South African International Boundary* (2002) ISBN 1-919798-41-2
27. *Mobile Namibia: Migration Trends and Attitudes* (2002) ISBN 1-919798-44-7
28. *Changing Attitudes to Immigration and Refugee Policy in Botswana* (2003) ISBN 1-919798-47-1
29. *The New Brain Drain from Zimbabwe* (2003) ISBN 1-919798-48-X
30. *Regionalizing Xenophobia? Citizen Attitudes to Immigration and Refugee Policy in Southern Africa* (2004) ISBN 1-919798-53-6
31. *Migration, Sexuality and HIV/AIDS in Rural South Africa* (2004) ISBN 1-919798-63-3
32. *Swaziland Moves: Perceptions and Patterns of Modern Migration* (2004) ISBN 1-919798-67-6
33. *HIV/AIDS and Children's Migration in Southern Africa* (2004) ISBN 1-919798-70-6
34. *Medical Leave: The Exodus of Health Professionals from Zimbabwe* (2005) ISBN 1-919798-74-9
35. *Degrees of Uncertainty: Students and the Brain Drain in Southern Africa* (2005) ISBN 1-919798-84-6
36. *Restless Minds: South African Students and the Brain Drain* (2005) ISBN 1-919798-82-X
37. *Understanding Press Coverage of Cross-Border Migration in Southern Africa since 2000* (2005) ISBN 1-919798-91-9
38. *Northern Gateway: Cross-Border Migration Between Namibia and Angola* (2005) ISBN 1-919798-92-7
39. *Early Departures: The Emigration Potential of Zimbabwean Students* (2005) ISBN 1-919798-99-4
40. *Migration and Domestic Workers: Worlds of Work, Health and Mobility in Johannesburg* (2005) ISBN 1-920118-02-0
41. *The Quality of Migration Services Delivery in South Africa* (2005) ISBN 1-920118-03-9